Conservation Heroes

JANE GOODALL

Conservation Heroes

Ansel Adams
John James Audubon
Rachel Carson
Jacques Cousteau
Jane Goodall
Al Gore
Steve and Bindi Irwin
Chico Mendes
John Muir
Theodore Roosevelt

Conservation Heroes

JANE GOODALL

Tara Welty

CHELSEA HOUSE

An Infobase Learning Company

JANE GOODALL
Copyright © 2011 by Infobase Learning

Chelsea House
An imprint of Infobase Learning
132 West 31st Street
New York, NY 10001

Library of Congress Cataloging-in-Publication Data
Welty, Tara.
    Jane Goodall / Tara Welty.
        p. cm. — (Conservation heroes)
    Includes bibliographical references and index.
    ISBN 978-1-60413-952-5 (hardcover)
    1. Goodall, Jane, 1934– —Juvenile literature. 2. Primatologists—England—
Biography—Juvenile literature. 3. Chimpanzees—Research—Juvenile literature.
4. Women conservationists—England—Biography—Juvenile literature. I. Title.
    QL31.G58W45 2011
    333.72092—dc22
    [B]   2010030583

Text design by Annie O'Donnell
Cover design by Takeshi Takahashi
Composition by Newgen North America
Cover printed by Yurchak Printing, Landisville, Penn.
Book printed and bound by Yurchak Printing, Landisville, Penn.
Date printed: April 2011
Printed in the United States of America

10 9 8 7 6 5 4 3 2 1

This book is printed on acid-free paper.

Contents

An Amazing Discovery

One word to describe Jane Goodall would be *patient*. For three months in the fall of 1960, 26-year-old Goodall camped in the forests of Gombe, Tanzania (then Tanganyika). She was there to observe the wild chimpanzees, but there was a problem: The chimpanzees had never seen a white human before. They would not let her come near. Yet Goodall was patient. It was one of the reasons she was selected for this job.

Day after day, week after week, Goodall climbed to the top of the same rocky peak, sat in the same spot, and waited. On a good day, some chimpanzees appeared in the valley below. Goodall watched them through her binoculars and wrote down her observations. After the chimps left the area, Goodall would go down to the valley and collect scraps of the chimps' discarded food. Goodall learned a lot this way, but she hoped for more. She wanted to see up close how the chimpanzees lived.

One day, Goodall was on her way up to the peak when a sudden movement caught her eye. She stopped dead in her tracks, ducked

British anthropologist and primatologist Jane Goodall, seen here in 1974, is known for her quiet, patient interactions with chimpanzees.

down into the grass, and raised her binoculars. Through the view-finder, Goodall saw a single chimpanzee sitting atop a termite mound. She recognized the chimp by the distinctive gray patch of fur beneath his chin. She had seen him before; he was one of the few chimps that was not afraid of her. Goodall had given this chimp a name: David Greybeard.

Goodall watched as David Greybeard picked up a long blade of grass and dipped it into the sandy termite mound. He then stuck the blade of grass into his mouth. He repeated this over and over. When David Greybeard had left the area, Goodall walked over to the mound. She picked up a blade of grass and did as David had done. When Goodall removed the grass, the blade was covered in

Chimpanzees are able to use tools in a way similar to humans, as exemplified by the chimps using sticks to fish for termites in this image from Uganda.

ANIMALS THAT USE TOOLS

People use tools every day. We use many more tools than just hammers and saws. A tool is any object that is used to help accomplish a task. Pens, spoons, and even nail clippers are all human tools.

Thanks to Jane Goodall and other animal researchers, we now know that animals in the wild use tools. Goodall was the first to observe wild chimpanzees using tools. She also spotted another tool-user in Tanzania–the Egyptian vulture. Egyptian vultures like to eat ostrich eggs. However, the shells are very tough and hard to crack. Goodall observed vultures using rocks to break open the eggs. The rocks were used as tools.

Another animal that uses a rock as a tool is the sea otter. Sea otters eat shellfish, but they are not physically strong so they need

termites. David had been using the grass to "fish" for termites. He was using the blade of grass as a tool.

Over the next few days, Goodall observed more chimpanzees "termite fishing." Sometimes the chimpanzees chose leafy twigs to use as "fishing poles." They stripped the leaves from the twigs before using them. Seeing the chimpanzees do this was an even bigger discovery. Not only did the chimps *use* tools, they actually *made* them! This discovery changed the way scientists thought about chimpanzees, humans, and the entire animal kingdom.

REDEFINING MAN

Today we know that several kinds of animals use tools. In 1960, that was not known. Back then, scientists believed that humans were the only animals that could make and use tools. In fact, humans were

another way to break open the hard shells of the shellfish to get to the meat inside. A rock is the perfect tool to do this. When they have food to eat, sea otters float on their backs and place a rock on their chests. They then use the rock to crack open the shellfish.

Recently, scientists have found that yet another animal may use tools: the octopus. An octopus's favorite tool is a coconut shell. When an octopus finds a coconut shell on the ocean floor, it picks up the shell, cleans it, and carries it away. When a predator is nearby, the octopus climbs inside the shell to stay out of sight. The coconut shell makes a great hiding place.

Many animals use tools, but chimpanzees are still the all-time champions of tool use. For example, they use leaves to collect water, large sticks to protect themselves from enemies, and rocks to crack open nuts. Chimpanzees use tools for more purposes than any other animal except for humans.

nicknamed "Man the Toolmaker" as a way to separate them from other animals.

Goodall sent a telegram to prominent paleontologist Dr. Louis Leakey to tell him about what she had seen. It was Leakey who had sent Goodall on her mission to Gombe. Leakey was thrilled with Goodall's discovery. He famously replied, "Ah! We must now redefine tool, redefine man, or accept chimpanzees as human!"

Not everyone was so pleased with Goodall's discovery—nor were they ready to believe it. Goodall had been Dr. Leakey's personal secretary before being assigned to Gombe. She had never been to college and had no formal scientific training. Many scientists criticized Goodall and Dr. Leakey. They did not believe that an "amateur" could make such an important discovery. In fact, some scientists accused Goodall of making up her observations. When Goodall was

(continues on page 14)

A CHIMP'S LIFE

Chimpanzees are the closest living relatives of human beings. In fact, humans and chimps share 95 to 98 percent of the same DNA. Check out pictures of chimpanzees. Do you recognize any "human-like" qualities?

When a baby chimpanzee is born, it clings to its mother's chest. It is helpless, a lot like a human baby. The mother nurses her baby and it sleeps with her in a nest high in the trees. When the baby is about three years old, it is ready to become more independent. It learns from its mother what fruits, nuts, and plants to eat and how to use twigs to "fish" for insects. It even learns to eat meat occasionally.

The young chimpanzee gets to know other members of its community. The others are very vocal—they grunt, scream, and drum on their chests to communicate. Each chimp has its own individual sound, called a pant-hoot, that sounds different from any other chimp. The young chimp has a pant-hoot, too.

The community helps care for the young chimpanzee. The other chimps help groom it and show it affection. They hug, hold hands, kiss, tickle, and pat the chimp. When the youngster is feeling playful, they chase it through the forest. The young chimpanzee might develop a close friendship with another young chimp. As adults, the two "best friends" will still do a lot of activities together.

Life is not always easy for the chimpanzee. Sometimes other chimps in its community and outside of it can become angry and violent. They can scream, hit, bite, and throw rocks. An adult chimp is five or six times stronger than a human being, so these outbursts can be dangerous.

The chimpanzee faces dangers outside of its community, too. The forests in Africa where it lives are being destroyed. Chimps are also hunted for meat and can become infected with the same

diseases that harm humans. Chimpanzees are an endangered species. There are fewer than 300,000 of them left in the wild. That is about the size of the population of Tampa, Florida. Conservationists such as Jane Goodall are working to protect wild chimpanzees and save them from extinction.

Chimpanzees typically socialize only with other chimps within their community.

(continued from page 11)

able to take photographs of the chimps termite fishing, many scientists remained unconvinced. Some even said that Goodall must have taught the chimps how to fish for termites.

In the end, Jane Goodall's observations of chimpanzees making and using tools were proved true. That meant that humans needed to be defined by other unique features, not just tool use. Goodall's discovery was an important one for our understanding of both humans and of animals in the wild. It was also important for Goodall personally. Because of her findings, Goodall received a grant from the National Geographic Society. With the new research funding, Goodall was able to remain in Gombe and continue studying the wild chimpanzees.

50 YEARS OF CONSERVATION

Goodall's big discovery of chimpanzee tool use happened more than 50 years ago. And it was this discovery that made Jane Goodall one of the most famous animal researchers in the world. Goodall went on to learn many more amazing facts about chimpanzees and their behavior. She learned that chimpanzees are playful and nurturing to their young, that they experience sadness, and that they care for one another. She also learned that chimpanzees can be violent and can attack others from outside their groups. Essentially she learned that chimpanzees are complex primates, much like human beings, to whom they are closely related.

Jane Goodall's discoveries led her to become an activist and conservationist, fighting to protect chimpanzee habitats, to stop the hunting of wild chimpanzees for meat, and to improve the lives of captive chimpanzees in laboratories and in zoos. About 25 years ago, Goodall left her research station at Gombe. Since then, she has traveled around the world—from small villages in Africa, to large conferences in Europe, to classrooms in the United States—telling her story and encouraging people to get involved to take better care of animals and our world.

A Curious Child

Valerie Jane Morris-Goodall was born in London on April 3, 1934. To her friends and family, she was nicknamed "V.J." Later, she would come to be called simply "Jane." Goodall has said that from the moment she was born, the events in her life seemed to steer her toward her eventual career of observing chimpanzees.

The first of these events came when Jane was just one year old. That year, Jane's father bought her a gift that would be a preview of her life to come. It was a stuffed chimpanzee named Jubilee. Jane's mother, Vanne, hated the toy chimp and thought it would scare young Jane. It didn't. In fact, Jubilee became Jane's favorite toy; she carried it everywhere and spent all her time with the chimp nearby. Many years later, many people thought it would be scary for a young woman to go into the wilds of Africa to spend all her time with chimpanzees. Just as she had with Jubilee, Jane proved everyone wrong. She also kept Jubilee, and to this day the well-loved chimp sits on a shelf in her home.

The next telling event happened at around the same time, when Jane was still a toddler. Even at a young age, she was fascinated with animals. Vanne encouraged Jane to explore the world around

15

Jane Goodall's father gave her this stuffed toy chimpanzee named Jubilee for her first birthday. In an interesting foreshadowing of her life's work, it became young Jane's favorite toy.

her. One day, Jane came in from the garden with a handful of earthworms. She climbed into her bed with the squirmy creatures. In a 2003 speech, Goodall remembered her mother's reaction, "She didn't even freak out . . . she just gently said, 'Jane, if you leave them here, they'll die. They need the earth.'" Jane thought for a moment. She had wanted to bring the worms inside because she loved them.

She didn't want them to die, so she picked up the worms and returned them to the garden. That day, Jane learned a valuable lesson: To really care for an animal, it is important to let it live as nature intended. This is a lesson that Jane would remember all her life.

A third important event came when Jane was four. On a visit to her grandmother's farm, Jane had the responsibility of collecting eggs from the henhouse. Jane saw the hens go into the henhouse. When they came out, each hen had left a precious new egg behind. This confused Jane. How exactly did the hens lay the eggs? Jane decided to find out for herself.

Jane waited outside the henhouse. When one of the hens entered the henhouse, Jane followed it. The hen was immediately frightened by Jane and squawked its way out of the henhouse. Other children might have given up, but Jane came up with a plan. She went into another henhouse and waited patiently in the corner, out of sight. After some time, a hen came in to lay her egg. Jane crouched silently and watched.

In her 1999 book *Reason for Hope*, Goodall describes what happened next: "Filled with excitement . . . I ran home. It was almost dark—I had been in that small stuffy henhouse for nearly four hours . . . No one knew were I was, and the whole household had been searching for me. They had even called the police to report me missing." Jane might have gotten in trouble for disappearing and scaring her family, but Jane's mother saw her daughter's excitement at her discovery. Rather than scold her daughter, Vanne listened as Jane enthusiastically described what she had seen in the henhouse. From this experience, Jane learned that by being patient and observant, she could learn about the natural world.

THE WAR YEARS

On September 3, 1939, when Jane was five years old, Britain declared war on Germany and entered World War II. Her father enlisted in the army to join the fight, and Jane and her mother and sister moved in with Jane's maternal grandmother in Bournemouth, a coastal town

WORLD WAR II AND BRITAIN

Nazi Germany, under the leadership of Adolf Hitler, invaded Poland in September 1939. Two days later, France and Britain (the Allied forces) declared war against Germany (part of the Axis powers). World War II had begun.

At the beginning of the war, life continued as usual in Britain. People in London received gas masks to use in case of an attack, but they otherwise went on with their lives. In 1940, the British government began rationing food, gasoline, and other supplies because certain items were needed to prepare for a larger-scale war. People had to learn to make do with less in order to support the war effort.

In May 1940, Germany invaded France, Holland, and Belgium, and began dropping bombs on Britain. The British government sounded air-raid sirens to warn people when bombs would likely be dropping. People took cover in special shelters, or even in the subway system, and waited until it was safe. Many people's homes were destroyed in the bombings, so the government asked people to take in others who had lost their homes.

After Germany conquered France, the possibility of a British invasion became very real. In 1941 Germany and Britain fought a battle, which Britain narrowly won, avoiding a major invasion.

in southern England. They lived in a large brick house called the Birches. Joining them were Jane's two aunts and an uncle. Two more women who had lost their homes in the war later moved in as well. During the war, it was common for people to take in strangers who had become displaced.

Jane and her family had to adapt to a new lifestyle during the war. There were very few food and household supplies available throughout the country, so the government had to ration them out.

On December 7, 1941, Japanese forces bombed the U.S. Navy base at Pearl Harbor, Hawaii. This prompted the United States to declare war on Japan and join the Allied Powers. Many U.S. troops were stationed in Britain during the war. With additional forces, the Allied Powers began to gain ground against the Axis powers. Jane Goodall often saw soldiers on the streets of Bournemouth. They usually had a bit of candy or chocolate to give away to the local children.

In 1943, news spread that the Nazis had been rounding up Jewish people (and others against whom they discriminated) and sending them to concentration camps. There they were starved, forced to work hard labor, and were murdered in mass numbers in gas chambers. In all, the Nazis killed 6 million Jews.

In early 1945, the concentration camp at Auschwitz was liberated. Over the next several months, people in other camps were set free. On May 7, Germany surrendered and ended World War II in Europe. May 8 is celebrated as VE (Victory in Europe) day in Europe.

The conflict between the United States and Japan continued. On August 6, the United States dropped an atomic bomb on Hiroshima, Japan. Three days later, they dropped another on Nagasaki. The Japanese surrendered on August 14, officially ending World War II.

People received government coupons for basic items such as eggs, milk, gasoline, and clothing. Even with coupons, sometimes these supplies were not available.

Germany heavily bombed England throughout the war. The British government used a loud air-raid siren to alert people when there was the threat of a bombing. Jane's family built an air-raid shelter in their home, and when the alarm sounded, everyone crouched in the shelter and waited until it was safe to come out.

Life during wartime is difficult. Jane was a small child when the war started, though, so this new way of life became normal to her. Many of Jane's experiences during the war years also helped shape her path toward a career with animals.

Escape Through Books

Jane loved reading. Whenever she felt angry or upset, she escaped into the fantasy world of books, which always cheered her up. In the winter, Jane read indoors, but in warmer weather she took her books outdoors. The backyard of the Birches was full of trees, and Jane loved to climb them and read her books perched high in the branches.

Jane especially loved books about animals. Her favorite was *The Story of Doctor Doolittle* by Hugh Lofting. The book's main character is a veterinarian who can talk to animals. In the story, Dr. Doolittle rescues a group of circus animals and takes them back to their native land in Africa. When she was a little older, Jane read *The Jungle Book* by Rudyard Kipling and *Tarzan of the Apes* by Edgar Rice Burroughs.

Tarzan especially caught Jane's imagination. In it, apes in Africa raise the human character, Tarzan. Eventually, Tarzan meets and falls in love with an American girl named Jane. *Tarzan and the Apes* was the first book in a whole series about Tarzan. Young Jane Goodall read them all. She had a big crush on the character of Tarzan and thought she would make a better girlfriend than his Jane.

Reading all of the Tarzan books gave Jane an idea. When she grew up, she would move to Africa and live among the animals. Many people told Jane that her plan was unrealistic. After all, the war was going on, and at the time not many women had serious careers. Additionally, Africa was thought of as a wild place, unsafe for a young woman. Even so, Vanne encouraged Jane's dreams. In a 2003 speech, Goodall remembered, "My mother used to say, 'Jane, if you really want something and work hard and you take advantage of every opportunity and you never, ever give up, you will find a way.' So that's how I grew up." Jane was determined to find a way to Africa.

KING OF THE JUNGLE

Jane Goodall has said that her girlhood crush on the character Tarzan inspired her to want to live in Africa. She was far from the only young person to be enchanted by Tarzan and his adventures in Africa. In fact, the character Tarzan is one of the most well-known and beloved characters in literature.

Edgar Rice Burroughs published the first Tarzan book, *Tarzan of the Apes,* in 1914—20 years before Jane Goodall was born. The book was so successful that Burroughs wrote 25 sequels to the original book, all of which Jane read.

In *Tarzan of the Apes,* a baby boy is stranded with his parents on the west coast of Africa. After the baby's parents are killed, apes adopt him and rename him Tarzan. The boy grows up in the jungles of Africa, swinging from the trees and going on great adventures with the jungle animals. As an adult, Tarzan meets an American girl named Jane and the two fall in love. When Jane goes back to civilization, Tarzan must decide whether to stay in the jungle with his animal family or go after her. He chooses to go after Jane and eventually the couple marries.

The Tarzan books inspired a whole series of spin-offs. The character Tarzan has starred in radio shows, television series, two Broadway plays, video games, and more than 85 movies, including a Disney film that was later made into a Broadway musical. No wonder Tarzan is known as the "King of the Jungle."

AFTER THE WAR

World War II ended in Europe on May 7, 1945, with the defeat of the Nazi forces. Pictures of Nazi concentration camps began to appear in local newspapers, showing starving prisoners and gas chambers where people were killed hundreds at a time. Suddenly, people around the world were forced to face the horrors of the war. These pictures deeply affected Jane, who was 11 years old at the time.

Jane thought a lot about the Nazis and what they had done to the Jews and other people they discriminated against. She wondered how any human being could behave so cruelly toward another. She also thought about other examples of human violence in history, such as the Spanish Inquisition and the African slave trade. These examples made her question why some people seemed truly evil, while others were good. These are questions she would continue to think about well into her adult life.

Divorced Parents

One year after the war ended, Jane's parents got divorced. Since Jane's father had been away fighting in the war, things did not change very much in her life. She continued to live at the Birches with her mother and sister.

The Alligator Club

Jane loved to play outdoors as much as she loved to read. The huge backyard at the Birches was a great place to explore nature. Jane spent hours in the backyard studying birds, snails, and insects. She even formed a nature club with her sister, Judy, and a few friends. It was called the Alligator Club.

Jane was the oldest and took charge of the club. She organized meetings and took the group on nature walks through the backyard. Jane recorded everything she saw on the walks. She even published an Alligator Club magazine with information about animals. In her 1996 book *My Life with the Chimpanzees*, Goodall remembers the magazine: "It was filled with nature notes, drawings of insect anatomy, and other such things. The other members were supposed to contribute, and make comments and suggestions—but they hardly ever did." For the other members, the Alligator Club was a fun way to hang out with friends, but for Jane it was an opportunity to record her observations about nature and prepare for her life in Africa.

A Girl's Best Friend

Jane had many pets growing up—cats, guinea pigs, a hamster, and tortoises, to name a few. However, her favorite pet did not really belong to Jane's family at all. It was a neighbor's dog, named Rusty. Jane has said that Rusty had a major impact on her understanding of animals.

Jane Goodall learned a lot about animals by observing and spending a great deal of time with Rusty (seen here with teen-aged Jane), a neighbor's dog.

Rusty lived at a hotel across the street from the Birches. The owners did not have a lot of time for a dog, so Jane took Rusty on walks. The two soon became inseparable. Rusty ran over to visit Jane at the Birches in the morning and barked to be let inside. He spent the whole day with Jane and returned home at night.

Jane loved to play with Rusty. She even liked to dress him up in human clothes. Jane taught Rusty to sit, roll over, and to catch a treat in his mouth. Rusty taught Jane that animals think and reason, that they can be loyal and loving, and that they have emotional lives. These are lessons that Jane carried with her all the way to Africa, lessons that she still carries with her today.

High School

Jane attended an all-girls high school. Although she received good grades, she didn't particularly enjoy school. She much preferred to do her learning through books and by studying nature herself. Although high school may not have been Jane's favorite place, it is where she became best friends with a girl named Marie-Claude Mange, Clo for short. Clo would later become a very important part of Jane's journey to Africa.

Jane graduated high school toward the top of her class. She was a smart young woman with a sense of adventure. There was only one problem: What should she do next?

Getting to Africa

After high school, Jane Goodall faced an uncertain future. Jane's mother, Vanne, did not have enough money to send her to college. At the time, scholarships were only available to students who spoke a foreign language. Goodall didn't, and so attending college was out of reach.

It was the 1950s, and there were few career opportunities available to women. As Goodall writes in her 1999 book *Reasons for Hope,* her mother suggested that she go to secretarial school because, "secretaries could get jobs anywhere in the world." Goodall's mother thought that she could use her secretarial skills to get a job in Africa one day, so the bright young woman with a love of animals moved to London to learn to be a secretary.

Goodall took full advantage of the big city life in London, visiting museums and art galleries and attending concerts. Living in the city was fun and exciting, but it was also expensive. Goodall had very little money, so after graduating from secretarial school, she returned to her hometown and got a job working for her aunt at a medical clinic.

Her aunt was a physical therapist who helped children with physical injuries or disabilities. Goodall's job at the clinic was to sit in on sessions with the doctor and write notes about the patient on medical charts. Though she only held this job for a few months, she has said that it affected her deeply. "I learned so much working at that clinic," Goodall notes in her 1996 book *My Life with the Chimpanzees*. "Ever since then, when things have gone wrong in my life, I remember how lucky I am to be healthy."

Goodall's next job was as a secretary at Oxford University. She then took a job in London selecting music for documentary films. She enjoyed the work, but she still dreamed of getting to Africa.

LONDON IN THE 1950s

The 1950s were boom times in London. After suffering devastating bombings during World War II, the city was ready to rebuild and come back bigger and stronger. Large numbers of workers were brought in from other cities to rebuild roads, schools, and hospitals. Since these new workers also needed places to live, new housing was built, too.

During this time manufacturing jobs were on the rise in the city. Workers in factories made televisions, washing machines, and other home appliances. These products made ordinary people's lives easier and more enjoyable.

Men had more opportunities in the workforce. While many women had taken on traditionally "male" work during the war, they were expected to give up their jobs to returning male soldiers. Many women were homemakers during this time. Other women, such as Jane Goodall, took another path. In the bustling city of London, more opportunities arose for young women to take on office work. In the 1950s, the number of women working in London offices surpassed the number of men for the first time.

LETTER FROM AN OLD FRIEND

On December 18, 1956, Goodall received a letter in the mail. In the upper corner of the envelope were two stamps, one with an elephant and one with two giraffes. The postmark was from the country of Kenya in Africa. She looked at the return address and saw it was from her best friend from high school, Clo Mange.

Mange's family had purchased a farm in Kenya. In the letter, Mange told Goodall about the farm and invited her to come for a visit. Goodall hadn't seen her friend since they had graduated high school, but Mange hadn't forgotten her. The trip would be a dream come true. Goodall had always wanted to travel to Africa. Now was her opportunity. She just had to find a way to pay for the ticket.

Saving Up

Goodall loved her job at the film company, but it did not pay very well. The cost of paying rent and living in London was eating up most of her meager salary. There was no way she could ever save up enough to go to Africa if she stayed in the city. Goodall decided that in order to save up enough money, she would need to return home to the Birches, where rent was free and expenses were low. Once again, the young woman said goodbye to glamorous city life and returned home to the country.

Back in Bournemouth, Goodall got a job as a waitress. She worked very hard, taking orders and carrying plates of food. The work was less interesting than working on films, but Goodall found ways to challenge herself. She tried to see how many plates she could carry on a tray at once without dropping them. Her record was 13 plates. Each weekend, Goodall stowed away her wages and tips, waiting for the day when she had saved up enough. After four months, Goodall counted up her earnings: She had enough money to go to Africa!

SET SAIL FOR A NEW LIFE

On March 13, 1957, Goodall said goodbye to her family and boarded a boat in London called the *Kenya Castle*. The boat sailed down the

The ocean liner *Kenya Castle*, which brought Jane Goodall from London to Kenya in 1957, held 526 passengers.

west coast of Africa, around the Cape of Good Hope, and up to Mombasa in Kenya.

The other passengers on the ship got seasick, but Goodall did not. She loved to stay up on the deck and look out over the vast ocean. She watched schools of dolphins and flying fish leap through the air above the water's surface and then plunge back into the depths. She even saw some shark fins circling the open ocean. In *My Life with the Chimpanzees*, Goodall writes, "I shall remember that wonderful voyage as long as I live."

The boat made a few stops along the way and Goodall got to step onto the soils of Africa for the first time. One of the stops was in the Canary Islands, the very place where Dr. Doolittle travels in

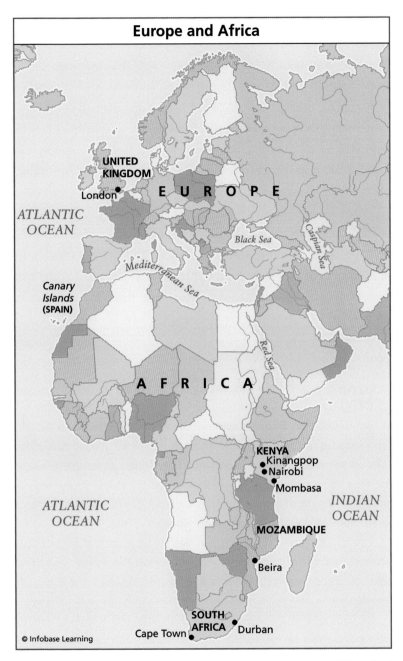

Europe and Africa

UNITED
KINGDOM
London
ATLANTIC
OCEAN
E U R O P E
Black Sea
Caspian Sea
Canary
Islands
(SPAIN)
Mediterranean Sea
Red Sea
A F R I C A
KENYA
Kinangpop
Nairobi
Mombasa
ATLANTIC
OCEAN
INDIAN
OCEAN
MOZAMBIQUE
Beira
SOUTH
AFRICA
Cape Town
Durban

© Infobase Learning

Goodall's long journey began by sea. From London, her ship sailed along the west coast of Africa with stops in the Canary Islands, Cape Town, Durban, Beira, and Mombasa, Kenya. Then, she and her family boarded a train in Mombasa traveling to Nairobi. Finally, they traveled in a Land Rover from Nairobi to Kinangpop.

the books Goodall read as a child. The place Goodall had imagined then suddenly became real before her eyes. Another stop was in Cape Town, South Africa. At the time, South Africa had a policy of apartheid, the legal separation of black Africans and white Africans. Seeing the poor treatment of black people deeply upset Jane. It reminded her of the discrimination Jews had faced during the war. Goodall believed that everyone should be treated equally, regardless of his or her background.

After 21 days at sea, with only a few stops, the boat finally arrived in Mombasa, Kenya. However, Goodall's journey was not over yet; she still had to travel by train to Nairobi, the capital city of Kenya. Goodall watched out the window of the train as the vast landscapes of Kenya spread out before her. After a two-day train

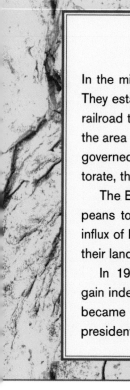

KENYA AND BRITAIN

In the mid-1800s, British explorers and traders traveled to Kenya. They established trading posts and later, in 1895, began to build a railroad to move goods across land. The British government made the area into a protectorate, which is a territory that is protected, or governed, by another country. They called it the East Africa Protectorate, though it was later renamed *Kenya*.

The British government encouraged its citizens and other Europeans to move to Kenya and start farms on the fertile land. The influx of Europeans forced the native people, called the Kikuyu, off their land.

In 1950s, a man named Jomo Kenyatta led a movement to gain independence for Kenya. After years of struggle, Kenya finally became independent in 1963. Kenyatta became the country's first president and the country was named after him.

ride, Goodall finally arrived in Nairobi on April 3. It was her twenty-third birthday.

A Wild Encounter

Clo and her family picked up Goodall at the train station. As Clo's father drove the group to the family farm, a large giraffe walked along the side of the road. Goodall had never seen a wild giraffe before. She studied the animal's distinctive markings and looked up at its long neck and large, peaceful eyes. She was absolutely amazed. Finally, she was in the place she had always dreamed about.

4

A New Work Opportunity

Being in Africa was Jane Goodall's dream come true. She saw wild animals such as hyenas and monkeys that she could have never seen roaming freely back home, and she explored beautiful landscapes that she had only imagined from reading books. In a letter to a friend in England, Goodall wrote, "Right from the moment I got here, I felt at home."

Goodall had a wonderful time visiting Clo at the Mange family farm in an area of Kenya called Kinangop. Not only did she get to enjoy nature out on the farm, but she also got to take advantage of city life in Nairobi. She and Clo went out in the evenings and often attended parties with other foreigners in the area. They had a wonderful time.

After three weeks, Goodall set out alone. Since she planned on being in Kenya for a while, she thought it would be rude to stay the whole time with her friend. She did not want to wear out her welcome. This is where her mother's advice of training as a secretary came in handy because she was able to move to Nairobi and take a secretarial job. The work was okay, but Goodall still hoped for an opportunity to work with animals.

The Aberdare Mountains are seen from the west in Kenya's Great Rift Valley. Jane Goodall felt at home in the beautiful, new setting.

That opportunity came at one of the parties she and Clo attended. Someone said to Goodall, "If you're interested in animals, you should meet Louis Leakey." Dr. Leakey was a well-known paleontologist and anthropologist at the natural history museum. He and his wife, Mary, would later become very famous when they discovered the fossilized remains of an early human ancestor.

AN APPOINTMENT WITH DESTINY

Goodall made an appointment with Leakey. She arrived at his office armed with a deep knowledge of Africa and its animals. Leakey was impressed and offered Goodall a job as his secretary. Goodall happily accepted, but there was a catch: The job would not start for several months because Leakey and his wife were planning a trip to Tanganyika (now Tanzania) to dig for fossils at Olduvai Gorge. Leakey promised that Goodall could begin her job when they returned.

Soon after arriving in Africa, Jane Goodall met famed anthropologist and paleontologist, Dr. Louis Leakey.

Before they left, Leakey took his newly hired secretary on a tour of Nairobi National Park. He shared stories about his life in Kenya and his experiences with the animals there. As Leakey got to know Goodall a little better, he decided he did not want to wait to hire her. He invited Goodall to come along on the trip to help dig for fossils at the gorge.

Trip to Olduvai Gorge

Goodall spent three months with the Leakeys at Olduvai Gorge. Today, the gorge is known as "The Cradle of Mankind" because of the amazing early human fossils that have been found there. When Goodall was there, only the local people called the Masai knew of it. The Leakeys were the first scientists to dig for fossils there.

Goodall was excited to be on a real adventure in the African bush. *Bush* is a word used to describe wild, uncultivated areas, and digging for fossils is difficult and exhausting in this setting. She worked alongside Mary Leakey. The two women spent long days in the hot sun, carefully chipping away at the soil with a pick or a hunting knife. When they came to a possible fossil, they used dental picks to gently excavate it. They had to take great care not to damage any fossils that might be beneath the soil. Any bone they found might be the next great discovery of a prehistoric creature.

After dinner each evening, the Leakeys and Goodall sat around the campfire and talked. There were no electric lights for miles and miles, and the stars shone brightly in the African sky. Louis Leakey talked a lot about how he wanted to understand the origins of human beings. He hoped to find answers buried in the soil at Olduvai. Goodall was fascinated by Dr. Leakey's stories.

One day, Leakey spoke to Goodall about his interest in the great apes—gorillas, chimpanzees, and orangutans. He explained that since great apes are primates and the closest relatives to human beings, their behavior might offer clues as to how early humans lived.

Leakey told Goodall that he knew of a group of chimpanzees living near Lake Tanganyika in what is now Tanzania. He was interested in sending someone there to study the chimps in the wild.

However, it would be a dangerous job because chimpanzees are very strong and can easily overpower a human being. Since their behavior in the wild was not well known, no one could predict how they would react to having a human around. The person who went on the study would have to be brave, patient, a quick thinker, and able to spend many hours alone in the wilderness. Goodall never imagined that Leakey would consider her fit for the task.

THE LEAKEYS AND NUTCRACKER MAN

When Jane Goodall met Louis and Mary Leakey, the couple was already well known for their digs at Olduvai Gorge. They had unearthed the fossils of mammals as well as stone tools, an indication that intelligent creatures related to humans once lived in the area. However, they were unsatisfied because they were determined to find the fossil remains of an early hominid, the ancestors to human beings.

In 1959 they did just that. Mary identified a small piece of bone in the ground. When she excavated it, she noticed that it was attached to some large, flat teeth—teeth that looked like they belonged to a hominid. The Leakeys continued the excavation, uncovering hundreds of skull fragments. The fragments were reconstructed into the skull of a creature with the scientific name of *Australopithecus boisei.* The Leakeys affectionately called it "Dear Boy." Researchers later began calling the creature "Nutcracker Man," because its wide, flat teeth suggested it ate nuts and seeds. New research, however, suggests that this is incorrect. The lack of wear on the teeth suggests it mostly ate plants and fruit.

Two years later, the Leakeys' son, Jonathan, found the remains of another hominid. Because this creature had a larger brain than Nutcracker Man, Dr. Leakey believed that it was a toolmaker. He gave it the scientific name of *Homo habilis,* or "man with skill." These two

Back in Nairobi

When the trip to Olduvai was over, Goodall continued to work at the museum with Leakey. The museum was filled with stuffed specimens of African animals. Sometimes Goodall went along on trips to collect specimens for the museum. Collecting specimens meant killing the animals and having them preserved by taxidermy. Goodall understood that this kind of collecting was necessary for

Louis Leakey and his family inspect the campsite of an early hominid in Olduvai Gorge, Tanzania, in October 1961.

important discoveries cemented the Leakeys as among the most important anthropologists in history.

Although Louis and Mary Leakey have both passed away, their children and grandchildren continue their legacy. The Leakey family remains committed to piecing together the story of our human ancestors.

scientific work at the museum; however, it wasn't what she had in mind when she had imagined a career working with animals. She wanted to work with live animals, not dead ones.

After she had worked at the museum for nine months, Goodall sent her mother a ticket to come and visit her in Nairobi. The woman who had encouraged her daughter to pursue the move to Africa would finally get to see her daughter living her dream.

NEW FOSSIL DISCOVERY

In 2007, a 9-year-old boy named Matthew Berger made an amazing discovery in South Africa. He found the fossilized collarbone of a new hominid species. Matthew's father, anthropologist Lee Berger, later found the creature's skull and other bones. They belonged to a young boy around Matthew's age who had lived nearly 2 million years ago. Berger and a team of researchers also found another skeleton from the same time, a female around 20 years old. There are additional fossils at the site that have yet to be unearthed.

The remains are the most complete set found from this time period and they are unlike any ever found before. The time period is important because this is when scientists believe the earliest human-like creatures lived on Earth. Just like the Leakeys, scientists today continue to look for fossils that provide a link to our earliest ancestors.

Scientists have named the new species *Australopithecus sediba*. They think that the creature had long, ape-like arms that allowed it to swing through the trees, but human-like legs so that it could walk upright and run through the forests. The fossils may provide clues to the mystery of human evolution. Then again, it may just be a creature that has long since gone extinct. It will

Goodall's mother had a great time in Kenya and enjoyed learning about the animals there.

During this time, Leakey continued to talk to Goodall about his hope to begin a study of the chimpanzees near Lake Tanganyika. The discussions frustrated Goodall because the work was exactly the kind of job she hoped to do. Yet, without a college degree, it seemed impossible. Finally, Goodall couldn't take it any more. According to

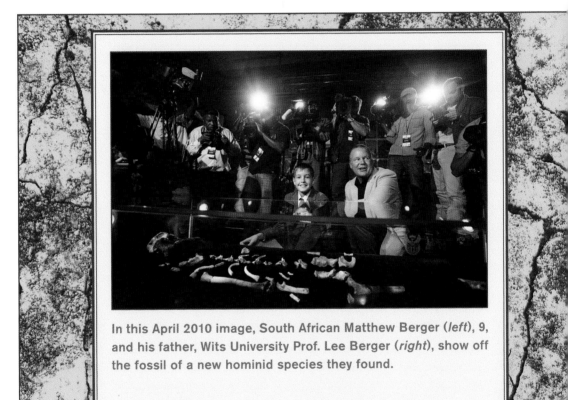

In this April 2010 image, South African Matthew Berger (*left*), 9, and his father, Wits University Prof. Lee Berger (*right*), show off the fossil of a new hominid species they found.

take years of more research and study of the fossils to know for sure.

For Matthew Berger, the fossils represent the first discovery of what he hopes will be many more. He wants to be a paleoanthropologist when he grows up. He is already well on his way.

Goodall's 1999 book, *Reasons for Hope*, she said to Leakey, "I wish you wouldn't keep talking about [the chimpanzee study] because that's just what I want to do." Leakey replied, "I've been waiting for you to tell me that." Leakey had had Goodall in mind for the study all along.

It wasn't as simple as just sending Goodall with a notebook and a pair of binoculars to the research site. Leakey needed to raise money to fund the study and get permission from the British government—because, at that time, Tanganyika was a protectorate of Britain—to do it. Although Leakey himself didn't care about Goodall's lack of education, he knew that many people in the scientific community would. He and Goodall agreed that if the study succeeded, Goodall would need to go back to college and earn a degree. They also agreed that she should travel back to England right away to learn as much as she could about chimpanzees before the study began. Goodall and her mother returned to England together. Goodall had spent one year in Africa.

RETURN TO ENGLAND

When Goodall arrived back in England, she had no idea of when or even if she would return to Africa to study chimpanzees. There was no guarantee that Leakey would be able to put the study together. A lot of very important pieces needed to fall into place. Still, she wanted to be prepared when the time came.

Goodall got a job at the London Zoo working in the television film library. She spent her free time at work watching the chimpanzees there. At the time, zoos were very different than how they are now. Today, most zoos try to replicate how animals live in the wild and provide them with enrichment activities to keep their minds stimulated. Back then, nobody paid much attention to how the animals naturally lived. The animals were kept in small cages and they were often alone. The London Zoo's male chimpanzee, named Dick, had been kept in his cage for a long time. He spent hours a day touching his fingertips together and opening and closing his mouth.

It seemed to Goodall that the chimpanzee had become crazed after so many years in a cage. It upset her to see the chimpanzee suffering in such conditions, and she vowed that one day she would help improve the lives of captive chimpanzees.

In addition to studying the chimps at the zoo, Goodall read many books about them. Most of the information she read was about captive chimps in labs or zoos. There was not much information available about chimps in the wild. That made Goodall even more excited to go into the wild and help collect information about chimpanzees.

In the meantime, Leakey worked on arranging the study. There were two big obstacles to overcome. The first was money. Although Leakey had great faith in Goodall's abilities, others didn't see her the same way. They saw her as an uneducated secretary with no experience. No one wanted to invest in a study that they believed would be a failure. Leakey persisted, though, and eventually raised the money.

The second big obstacle was getting permission. At the time, Tanganyika (now Tanzania) was a protectorate of Britain. That meant the British government would have to approve the study. The British government refused to allow one of their white female citizens to go alone into the African bush. They believed it was simply too dangerous. They would not approve the study unless Goodall agreed to take someone with her on the study. Luckily, Goodall's mother, Vanne, agreed to the task. She would travel with her daughter and stay with her in Tanganyika for three months.

ON HER WAY

Goodall and her mother flew to Nairobi. Together with Leakey, they prepared for the expedition. They collected camping gear, food, water, binoculars, clothing, and notebooks in which Goodall could record her observations. Finally, just as they were ready to depart, a problem arose. There was fighting among the local people in the area where Goodall was to travel. It was not safe for her to go there.

After more than a month of delays, Goodall and Vanne finally made it to Kigoma, the closest town to their destination. On July 16, 1960, the two women, along with a guide, boarded a small motorboat for a journey of 12 miles (19.31 km). As they cruised across the lake, they passed tiny fishing villages on the sandy shores. After about an hour, they came to the shores of the Gombe Game Reserve, what is now known as Gombe Stream National Park. This is where Goodall would conduct her study. Goodall looked around at the tall forests and tried to imagine her new life there. In *Reasons for Hope*, Goodall writes, "I already felt that I belonged to this new forest world, that this is where I was meant to be."

A Time of Discovery in Gombe

5

When Jane Goodall arrived at Gombe on July 16, 1960, there was a lot of work to do. The young researcher and her mother needed to find a place to set up camp, put up their tents, unpack their supplies, and get something to eat. The only thing Goodall wanted to do, however, was explore the land that would become her home.

The guide who was traveling with them found a shady spot near a stream for the women to set up their camp. They built a tent for Goodall and her mother, and a cook they had hired put up his own tent nearby and began to prepare dinner. Once all the work was done, Goodall left the group and set off into the forest on her own. It was getting late, and she didn't go far. Even so, she soon wandered right into a troop of baboons. The baboons were understandably afraid of this new creature in the forest, and they sounded a call of alarm to warn the other animals of the forest to stay away. Next Goodall came to a bushbuck, a kind of small deer. Again the animal was afraid. If all these animals were scared of her, Goodall thought, the chimpanzees probably would be, too.

The next morning, Goodall set out to search for chimpanzees with a local African guide. At first, she was not allowed to go into the forests of Gombe alone. She always had to be accompanied by a guide. This was one of the rules set up by the British government to protect the young researcher during her study. Goodall didn't really want to have a guide with her all the time, but she had to follow the rules.

Jane Goodall and her mother, Vanne, spend time in their tent near Gombe Stream in 1960.

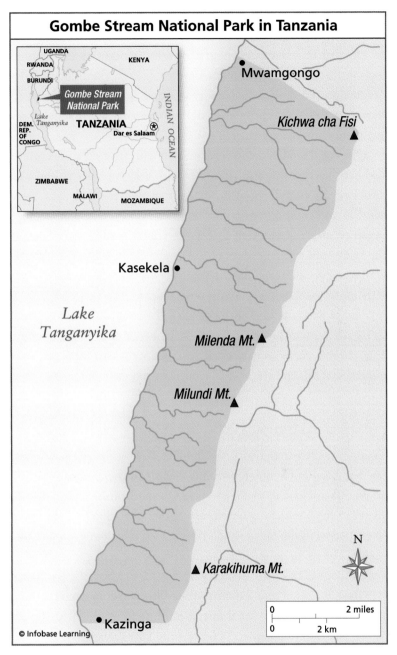

Gombe Stream National Park in Tanzania

Gombe Stream National Park is the smallest of Tanzania's national parks. Besides the chimpanzee habitat, there are a troop of beachcomber olive baboons, red-tailed and red colobus monkeys (the latter of which are regularly hunted by chimps), leopards, snakes, buffalos, and approximately 200 bird species.

On that first day out, Goodall and the guide saw two chimps high in the treetops. When the chimps spotted the humans, they became scared and rushed away, warning their fellow chimps as they went. Goodall continued searching every day, but she didn't see any more chimps for a week.

One day, Goodall came across a tree with fruit on it. The guide told her that this was one kind of fruit that chimps like to eat. The next day, she found a spot far away from the tree and went there early in the morning with her binoculars. Sure enough, chimps began to arrive at the tree to eat the fruit. Goodall went back to the same spot for three days to watch the chimps at the fruit tree. Unfortunately, however, her viewing spot was very far away so it was difficult to see much, even with binoculars.

Things went on this way for weeks. The chimps did not get used to having human beings around. That meant that Goodall could only observe them from a great distance. It wasn't what she had imagined at all, and she was learning less than she had hoped.

IN HER OWN WAY

Goodall was frustrated with the amount of progress she had made. She had been in Gombe for several weeks and the chimps were still afraid of her. Goodall made an appeal to the British game ranger to allow her to go searching for chimps on her own. She thought that a single person in the forest would be less intrusive than a team of two people. The game ranger finally agreed to let the young researcher go out on her own, as long as someone always knew where she was going.

Goodall settled into a daily routine: She woke up each morning at 5:30 A.M. and had a breakfast of toast and coffee. Then she set off to look for chimpanzees. Her favorite viewing spot was a high, rocky area she called "the peak." From the top of the peak, Goodall had a great view of the two valleys below. She watched the chimps in the valleys and, as she identified individuals, she gave each one a name. The names helped her keep track of which chimps did what activities. After the chimps had left the area, Goodall would climb

Each morning, Jane Goodall awoke at 5:30 A.M. and climbed up to the peak to watch the forests below and listen for the hoots and morning calls of chimpanzees.

down to where they had been. She would inspect the trees where the chimps had eaten and examine the items they left behind. In the evenings, she returned to her camp to have dinner with Vanne. Sometimes she would pick up supplies and leave again to camp overnight at the peak in order to be there bright and early in the morning.

Each day, Goodall learned something new from watching the chimpanzees. Over time, she began to understand more about their daily lives. Even so, Goodall worried about the project. There was only enough money to keep the study going for six months. She needed to quickly learn some important new information about chimps; otherwise, the project would be considered a failure.

A Mother's Support

Goodall's mother helped keep the camp during the day while Goodall was off with the chimps. Each evening, Goodall talked to Vanne about what she had learned in the forest. Even on nights when she camped at the peak, Goodall still came down to have dinner with her mother and talk about the day. She shared her successes, but also her frustrations and her worries about the project. In a 2009 interview with the nonprofit organization Academy of Achievement, Goodall explain that it helped to have a supportive person to listen when things were tough:

> My mother was amazing . . . she boosted my morale, because in those early days the chimpanzees ran away as soon as they saw me. They would vanish. [My mother] would say, in the evening when I was a bit despondent, "But think what you are learning. What they're feeding on. The kind of size groups they travel in. How they make beds at night, bending down the branches . . . ," all the things I'd seen through my binoculars. And so she boosted my morale.

Vanne did another important job in Gombe. She set up a small clinic for local people in the area. At the clinic, she gave out basic medical supplies such as aspirin and bandages that she had brought from England. People came from miles around to go to the clinic. Goodall has said that her mother's clinic helped establish a good relationship with the local people, a relationship that continues to this day.

It was helpful and comforting for Goodall to have her mother with her, but it couldn't last forever. Vanne had to get back to her life in England. After a few months, the British government agreed to allow Goodall to stay in Gombe on her own. Even though it was difficult for both of them, mother and daughter wished one another goodbye.

One Chimp Changes Everything

In early November 1960, about three months after her arrival in Gombe, Goodall made her first big discovery. Sitting at the peak, she spotted a chimp sitting on a termite mound. He had a white tuft of fur beneath his chin, so Goodall had given him the name "David Greybeard." David Greybeard was using a stick to "fish" for termites in the mound.

The next day, she saw David Greybeard again. This time he was with another chimp, Goliath. This time, David and Goliath made their own "fishing poles" out of modified twigs. This was proof that chimpanzees made and used tools.

A few days earlier, in October 1960, David Greybeard and Goliath provided Goodall with another important clue to chimpanzee behavior. Goodall observed the two chimps eating something. She strained to see what it was, and realized that it was some kind of meat. This was big news because it had always been believed that chimpanzees were vegetarians. Goodall later learned that chimpanzees hunted small monkeys and bush pigs.

David Graybeard visits Jane Goodall at her campsite.

David Greybeard continued to help Goodall with her study. One day in the summer of 1961, when Goodall returned to camp, the cook came to her with some news: A chimpanzee had visited the camp. The chimp had eaten some palm nuts from a nearby tree and had then stolen some bananas from the camp. Goodall wasn't upset about the lost bananas; she was excited about the visitor.

The next day, Goodall waited at camp for the chimp to return. She waited all day. Just when she thought the chimp would not show up, she heard a noise in the nearby bushes. She looked over and out came the chimpanzee—it was David Greybeard! He spotted some bananas at the camp and took them. For several more days, David Greybeard came back to camp to claim more bananas.

From then on, Goodall had a special relationship with David Greybeard. Sometimes in the forest he would come up to her, looking for a banana. The other chimpanzees saw David doing this. Because of him, the others were less afraid to have Goodall around. After all, they liked bananas, too.

A FAMOUS SCIENTIST

Goodall's discoveries about chimpanzees earned her a grant from the National Geographic Society to continue her research. National Geographic sent a documentary filmmaker named Hugo van Lawick to Gombe to film Goodall with the chimpanzees.

Van Lawick also shot photographs of Goodall with the chimps. In 1963 the pictures were published in *National Geographic* magazine, along with an article written by Goodall titled "My Life Among the Wild Chimpanzees." For the first time, the world read about the young English woman and her exciting adventures in the forests of Tanzania.

While van Lawick was on location in Gombe, he and Goodall fell in love. They were married on March 28, 1964. Van Lawick's film, *Miss Goodall and the Wild Chimpanzees,* was broadcast on U.S. television in 1965. It was a huge hit. Now people everywhere knew about Jane Goodall and her study of chimpanzees. Goodall

DIAN FOSSEY: FRIEND TO GORILLAS

Six years after Jane Goodall began her study of chimpanzees, another young researcher went into the forests of Africa to study great apes. Her name was Dian Fossey and she studied mountain gorillas. Like he had done for Goodall, Dr. Louis Leakey sent Fossey to begin her study.

(continues)

Primatologist Dian Fossey poses in front of an exhibit in 1984. Sent by Louis Leakey to Rwanda to study gorillas, Fossey was considered one of the foremost authorities on gorillas at the time of her death.

(continued)

Fossey was born in 1932 in San Francisco, California. Growing up, she had always had an interest in animals. Like Goodall, she dreamed of one day traveling to Africa. In 1963, at the age of 31, Fossey used her life savings to make the trip.

Fossey traveled to several countries in Africa. Along the way, she stopped at Olduvai Gorge and met Dr. Leakey. The famous researcher told her about Goodall's work with chimpanzees and said he believed that there should be more field studies done of the different great apes. It was on that trip that Fossey decided she wanted to study mountain gorillas.

Back home, Fossey published some articles about gorillas along with pictures of her trip. In 1966, Dr. Leakey traveled to the United States to give a lecture. Fossey attended and took the opportunity to show Dr. Leakey some of her articles. He was so impressed that he invited Fossey to take part in a gorilla study.

In December of that year, Fossey headed back to Africa to begin her study. She first stopped at the Gombe Stream Research Center and met with Goodall. Then she headed to Congo (then called Zaire) to set up her own research station.

At first, the gorillas were scared of Fossey. She began to imitate their movements and vocal sounds in order to make them feel

continued to star in documentaries for television and share the stories of Gombe's chimps with the world.

Being a famous scientist meant that Goodall had many more people examining her project. Often, they looked at it with a critical eye. Many scientists questioned Goodall's credentials. They thought that a woman without a college degree was not qualified for the job. They also questioned her research practices, especially her practice of giving names to the chimpanzees. Common

more comfortable. Eventually the gorillas accepted her as part of their group. She learned a lot about gorilla behavior this way.

In 1967, the political situation in Zaire became dangerous, so Fossey moved her study to Rwanda. She set up the Karisoke Research Center there. Again, Fosse had to introduce herself to the gorillas and establish a relationship with them. Over time, Fossey noticed that poachers were killing gorillas in the region. Gorillas were also threatened by the expansion of cattle herding into their forest homes. Fossey began a campaign to fight the poachers and cattle herders. Sometimes she confronted them directly. This made her unpopular with many of the local people.

In 1977, a poacher killed one of Fossey's favorite gorillas, Digit. Fossey went to the public and shared Digit's story. She also started a fund to raise money to save the mountain gorillas. Today, that fund is called the Dian Fossey Gorilla Fund International (DGFI). In 1983, Fossey published a book titled *Gorillas in the Mist* about her amazing time with the mountain gorillas. It was adapted into a 1988 film staring Sigourney Weaver.

Tragically, Dian Fossey's life was cut short. In 1985, she was murdered in her home in Rwanda. It is widely believed that Fossey was killed by the poachers who she had fought to keep from killing the gorillas. However, her murder has never been solved.

scientific practice was to assign numbers, not names to research subjects. By giving them names and discussing individual personality traits, many scientists thought that Goodall had become too personally connected to the chimps. Therefore, they argued, her research findings may not be valid. At the time of her study, Goodall didn't know much about common research practices, and she is now glad she didn't. She argues that she collected much more valuable information about chimps by studying them in her own way. Today, many scientists follow Jane Goodall's model in their own wild-animal studies.

ATTENDING CAMBRIDGE

After Goodall had been in Gombe for about 18 months, she received a letter from Louis Leakey. He wrote to let Goodall know that although he supported her research, he would not always be around

CONTROVERSY: NAMES VERSUS NUMBERS

No one would think twice about giving a name to a pet cat or dog. In fact, when Jane Goodall began naming the chimpanzees of Gombe, it was her childhood dog Rusty, along with other childhood pets, that had inspired the idea.

Lots of people in the scientific community, however, did think twice about Jane Goodall's chimpanzee names. This was especially true of Goodall's professors at Cambridge. When she first arrived at the school, Goodall was told that she had done everything incorrectly in her fieldwork. By naming the chimps, Goodall was told, she was assigning "human" attributes to the animals. Goodall's teachers told her that she should give the chimps numbers instead.

Goodall was also criticized for writing about the emotions of the chimpanzees. Most scientists of the day thought that animals could not have feelings, and even if they did, there was no way Goodall could know what they were. "When I talked about chimps having personalities and frames of mind, I was berated soundly," she recalled in a 2010 interview with the *Minneapolis Star-Tribune*. Goodall thought that this thinking was silly because she had witnessed animal emotions with her own pets as a child.

to help her get funding. Goodall would need to build her own credentials as a scientist. That meant she would need to go to school and earn a degree.

Based on her successful fieldwork, Leakey arranged for Goodall to be admitted to the Ph.D. program at Cambridge University. This was a huge accomplishment because very few people have ever been admitted to the program without first getting a bachelor's degree. Goodall left Gombe and set off for Cambridge.

In a 2009 interview with the nonprofit organization Academy of Achievement, Goodall spoke about how she reacted to her critics. She said that she thought about something her mother had once said to her. "She taught me that if you meet someone who disagrees with you, the first thing you do is listen, then you think," she said. So Goodall listened to her professors' opinions and suggestions. One professor, Robert Hind, had a strong effect on Goodall. Hind taught Goodall that she could not directly say if an animal felt a certain emotion because she could not really know for sure the feelings of anyone, whether human or chimpanzee. However, she could make educated guesses about a chimp's emotions based on its behavior. So Goodall learned to describe the chimps as behaving "as if" they felt a certain emotion instead of stating concretely that they did feel it.

Goodall held firm to her conviction that the chimps should be named and not numbered. By listening to her professors' arguments and combining their ideas with her own, Goodall developed a more sound and widely accepted set of research methods. Today it is common practice for researchers to interpret how an animal is feeling based on observation of its behavior. This is largely due to Goodall's approach to observing the chimpanzees.

When she arrived, Goodall was excited and nervous. She did not know what to expect since she had been out of school for several years. All of the other Ph.D. candidates had done their studying in college; she had done hers in the forests of Gombe.

At first, Goodall had a difficult time at Cambridge. Her professors told her that she had done her fieldwork in Gombe all wrong. She was criticized for giving the chimps names instead of numbers and for writing about their emotions. She had to work hard to convince her teachers otherwise.

In 1965, Goodall earned her degree in ethology, the study of animal behavior. Now that people could no longer question her credentials, the newly named Dr. Jane Goodall was ready to return to Gombe and continue her work.

Meet Gombe's Famous F Family

When Jane Goodall first went to Gombe, there were three main communities of chimpanzees. Goodall focused her research on the Kasakela community, which made its home in the Kasakela and Kakombe valleys. Goodall could observe them from her perch up at the top of the peak between the two valleys. To the north lived the much larger Mitumba community. To the south was the powerful Kalande community.

Goodall recorded in great detail the lives of the chimps in the Kasakela community, especially the members of the powerful F Family, headed by an old female named Flo. Goodall shared the stories of the individuals in this family and within the entire community in her *National Geographic* articles, documentaries, and books. Her accounts of chimpanzee society had all the elements of a dramatic soap opera—births and deaths, family drama, struggles for power, jealousy, and even violence. People all over the world tuned in eagerly to find out what was happening in the lives of the Gombe chimps. Research of the community continues today.

IT ALL STARTED WITH FLO

After David Greybeard started to visit Goodall, a few other chimps began to follow his lead. One was David's best friend and the leader of the community, Goliath. Another was named William. A third was a female who became especially important to Goodall's research. Her name was Flo. To human eyes, Flo was not an attractive chimpanzee. She had a large, bulbous nose, ragged ears, and teeth worn down to the gums. To other chimps, none of that mattered. Flo was one of the most popular females of the entire community.

Flo was the matriarch of one of the most powerful chimpanzee families in Gombe's history. Goodall gave each member of Flo's family a name beginning with the letter *F*. The F Family taught Goodall a lot about how members of the same chimp family interact and care for one another.

A Caring Mother

Flo brought her young daughter Fifi and juvenile son Figan with her to Goodall's camp. Flo also had an older adolescent son, Faben, who sometimes visited the camp, too. Flo was a patient and caring mother to little infant Fifi. She calmed Fifi when she was upset, and taught her the ins and outs of grooming. She was tough, too, offering discipline if Fifi acted out. She was also playful and often ran and played games with Fifi. When Flo was busy or not in the mood to play, big brother Figan stepped in to help keep Fifi entertained. The siblings enjoyed a close relationship.

When Fifi was about four years old, Flo began to wean her from nursing. She also stopped allowing Fifi to ride on her back and made her sleep in her own nest at night. This was not unusual. It is a process that all chimpanzees go through with their offspring at this age. It is an especially difficult and confusing time for the infant chimps, because they have to learn to become more self-sufficient and rely less on their mothers. Fifi was no exception. She became less playful and seemed depressed during the time that Flo was weaning her.

Soon after Fifi was weaned, Flo's body was ready to become pregnant once again. Goodall knew this because Flo's rear end swelled up and turned bright pink. Because she was such a popular

Flo was one of the first females to follow David Greybeard to the Goodall campsite in 1961. Soon after, many males began following her there, making the task of studying them much easier.

female, plenty of male suitors hoped to be the father of Flo's next offspring. They eagerly followed her around the forest. One day, Flo entered Goodall's camp just as she had done many times before, but

CROSSING COMMUNITIES

In chimpanzee society, males are dominant over females. There is one male in charge of all of the others. He is called the "alpha male." The male chimpanzees spend a lot of time patrolling the borders of their communities. They are trying to protect their territories from being taken over by chimpanzees from other communities. When they come into contact with males from other communities, sometimes violent battles will occur. Some of the chimps may even be killed.

Although male chimpanzees stay at home and protect their communities, female chimpanzees may cross into other communities without harm. They do this to mate with males in other communities. Often the females return home when they are done mating, but sometimes they join the other groups and live with them. The reason is a matter of survival for both communities. Each female in a community mates and produces offspring with several different males over the course of her lifetime. Within a small community, it becomes impossible to have a diverse gene pool if there are never any new members within a community. That is why it is important for females to be able to produce offspring with males from other communities.

Today, chimpanzee ranges are being divided into smaller and smaller geographic areas by roads, agricultural sites, and human communities. Each area may only be large enough for one community of wild chimpanzees. It is therefore much more difficult for female chimps to leave one community and join another. Scientists worry that isolating communities in this way will lead to genetic defects caused by inbreeding.

this time a large group of males followed her. (Once at the camp, the male chimps discovered Goodall's plentiful banana supply. From then on, the camp was often teaming with chimps, who enjoyed the tasty treats that Goodall happily provided.) The big males had been too cautious to enter the camp before, but they could not resist the chance to spend time with Flo. One by one, Flo allowed the males to mate with her. This is how Goodall discovered that female chimps mate with several males in a community during the same reproductive cycle. It is therefore nearly impossible without DNA testing to tell which male is the father of which infant. Male chimpanzees will work to protect all of the infants in the community because any one of the infants could be offspring of any of the male chimps.

FLO TEACHES HER OFFSPRING

When Goodall returned to Gombe from Cambridge in 1965, Flo had just given birth to a new baby named Flint. Fifi was now 6 years old and Figan was 11. They still spent all of their time with their mother. Older brother Faben wasn't around as much; he was off patrolling the territory, but he often returned to visit.

Baby Flint

Just as she had been to Fifi, Flo was an excellent mother to newborn Flint. She nursed Flint and carried him around clutched close to her stomach. Sometimes she relaxed on her back, stretched out her legs above her, and dangled the baby from her foot, tickling Flint until he was in a giggling fit. None of the other chimpanzee mothers played with their children in quite this way.

Fifi was amazed by her new brother. When Flint was four months old, Flo allowed Fifi to take a more active role in caring for her little brother. She groomed him, tickled him, and played games with him. Sometimes she even carried him through the forest, with Flo always close by. She tried to dangle him from her foot like her mother had done, but she was too small to support Flint's weight. By helping Flo care for Flint, Fifi was learning an important lesson herself—how to be a good mother.

By the time he was six months old, Flint had learned to walk on his own and climb trees. Instead of clinging to Flo's stomach, Flint rode around on her back. Flint spent more and more time playing with his older brothers, Faben and Figan. By interacting with them, Flint was learning the responsibilities of chimpanzee males to guard and protect the community. Flint also spent time with other youngsters his own age. If any other chimp became aggressive with Flint, Flo charged in and protected her son. The result was that Flint was confident and a little bit aggressive, or as Goodall describes him, "a spoiled brat."

A SAD END FOR AN OLD FRIEND

In 1966 an epidemic of polio swept through the Kasakela community. Chimpanzees are at risk for catching the same diseases as humans, and an outbreak of infectious disease can wipe out entire communities. In the outbreak of 1966, 15 of the chimps in the community became ill with the disease, and 6 died from it. The survivors suffered the effects of the disease for the rest of their lives.

Flo's eldest son, Faben, was one of the chimps affected by the polio outbreak. He lost the use of one arm and remained crippled his entire life. Goodall's old friend, David Greybeard, was also affected. One day in 1968 he stopped coming to camp altogether. After weeks and months of waiting for him to return, Goodall had to assume that David Greybeard had died. His body was never found.

David Greybeard's death was particularly difficult for Goodall. After all, David had been the chimp who had first given Goodall a glimpse into the private world of wild chimpanzees. Because of his calm and unafraid attitude, Goodall's study of him was possible. In her 1999 book *Through a Window*, Goodall writes of David's death: "I felt a sorrow deeper than that which I have felt for any other chimpanzee before or since." Despite her sadness, it was important for Goodall to continue her research.

NEW AMBITIONS AND NEW ADDITIONS

When Goodall first began observing the Gombe chimps, Goliath was the top-ranking male in the Kasakela community. To take the top spot in the community, male chimps must first challenge and dominate all the females in the community, then they must challenge each of the males individually. The top-ranking chimp must prove that he is the biggest and toughest of them all.

In order to win these challenges, each male develops his own "charging display." First, he stands his hair on end to appear bigger than he actually is, and then he picks up large branches and shakes them vigorously, or hurls the largest rocks he can find at his opponent. He stamps his feet and screams loudly. If none of that works, he may engage in a physical fight.

When Flo's son Figan was 11 years old, a chimp named Mike took the top spot away from Goliath. Mike had developed a unique charging display, using a human object and adapting it for a chimp purpose. He found empty 4-gallon (15-liter) tin cans in the camp and used them to his advantage. He picked up the tin cans and hurled them at his opponents. The noisy cans made quite a racket and scared off many rivals, leaving Mike free to take over as leader.

Figan was fascinated by Mike's strategy. He seemed to have ambition, even at that young age, to one day take over as top-ranking chimp. He wouldn't have to worry too much about a challenge from older brother Faben. Without the use of one arm, Faben was no longer stronger than his kid brother. Figan began practicing hurling the cans when there were no adults around to take them away. Goodall, however, removed all the cans from Gombe to protect the chimps, so Figan would miss out on using this strategy. He would have to find another way to dominate the others and become the leader.

Weaning Goes Awry

Just as she had with Fifi, Flo began weaning Flint when he was about four years old. This time, however, the weaning process did not go smoothly. Flo was very old at the time. Her teeth were worn down to the gums and her hair was thinning. She did not have the energy to push Flint away when he insisted on feeding with her. When Flint threw tantrums and whined, Flo usually gave in and let him have his way.

Flo also gave in when Flint insisted on riding around on her back like an infant. It was difficult for Flo's old body to move through the forest saddled with Flint, but she did not seem to have the energy to force his independence. Flo even let Flint push himself into her nest at night. She just let the spoiled brat have his way. This became especially problematic when Flo once again became pregnant.

New Baby Flame

In 1968, three years after Goodall returned from earning her Ph.D. at Cambridge, Flo gave birth to a baby named Flame. Flint was still unusually dependent on his mother and insisted on sleeping in the nest with Flo and Flame. He even forced Flo to carry him around on her back while she was carrying Flame against her stomach. It was a real struggle for the aging Flo to carry around her two young sons with her. Flo's old body was not strong enough to handle the task.

Six months after Flame was born, Flo became ill with a disease similar to pneumonia. She became very weak and frail. At night, she was not strong enough to climb into her nest, where she could rest safely in the trees with Flame. Instead, she slept on the ground, where it was much less comfortable and less safe. One day, Goodall found Flo lying on the ground. The infant Flame had disappeared and was never seen again.

After Flo recovered, Flint continued to act like an infant. Flo, possibly distraught over the loss of baby Flame, did not try to stop him from riding on her back or sleeping in the nest. This continued until Flint was eight years old and Flo was too old and weak to support his weight any longer.

THE NEXT GENERATION

When Fifi reached adolescence, she developed the natural urge to mate with the male chimps. Sometimes she mated with chimps in her own community. Other times she left her community for weeks at a time to join with males in another community. At the end of her mating period, she always returned to her mother and brothers in the home range. This continued for two years. Fifi was learning the independence needed to become the matriarch of her own family.

Fifi Becomes a Mother

In 1971, Fifi gave birth to her first baby, a boy named Freud. Over the course of her lifetime, Fifi had seven more babies: Frodo, Fannie, Flossi, Faustino, Ferdinand, Fred, and Flirt. Just as her own mother had been, Fifi was a caring and patient mother. She enjoyed spending time with her little infant. One day, she was even observed dangling little Freud from her foot and tickling him, the same thing Flo had done with baby Flint. Fifi had learned well from her mother.

Fifi and her baby, Flirt, are among the chimps living in Gombe Stream National Park.

DO GOOD MOTHERS MATTER?

In a 2009 interview with the nonprofit organization Academy of Achievement, Goodall said, "One of the things I loved learning most is chimp maternal behavior, because we find, just as in human society, there are good mothers and bad mothers." She went on to talk about the effects that each mother has on her children. Chimps with good mothers go on to be successful within their communities; chimps with bad mothers do not.

Flo is an example of a good mother. She was affectionate and tolerant, but also willing to discipline her children, at least before she became too old to do so. If any of her children were in trouble, she rushed to their aid, even if that meant putting herself in danger. The results were that Faben, Figan, Fifi, and Flint grew up to be self-confident and assertive. Figan went on to become the alpha male of his community. Fifi went on to become a high-ranking female and a good mother in her own right.

In stark contrast to Flo was another mother, Passion, who lived in the Kasakela community at the same time. Passion was

By this time, Flo was very old and did not show much interest in her grandson. She had enough difficulty trying to care for seven-year-old Flint, who still refused to grow up and become independent.

A New Alpha Male

Mike held the position of alpha male in the Kasekala community for six years. Toward the end of his reign, he was beginning to look old and tired. His hair was thinning and his teeth were worn down or broken. There were plenty of younger, stronger chimps who could have taken his place in the top spot. The top contenders were two

often tense and on edge. She did not like to spend time with the other females in the community. Passion was intolerant with her daughter, Pom. She did not play with the infant and did not seem to want to spend much time with her. As a result, Pom grew up edgy and insecure. She did not develop well socially with the other chimps and she did not grow up to be a good mother herself.

As Pom grew older, she and Passion developed a closer relationship. This was especially true after Pom's first baby, Pan, died in an accident. However, even as they grew closer to one another, Passion and Pom became more isolated from the other members of the community. They even worked together to commit violent acts against other chimps. Years later, after her mother died, Pom left the community for good.

Goodall believes that good mothers do matter. Just as Vanne had helped support and encourage Goodall, Flo helped support and encourage her own children. As a result, Flo's children were largely successful. Passion, on the other hand, did little to support her children. As a result, they were not successful.

brothers, Hugh and Charlie, who worked together as a team; Humphrey, who weighed at least 20 pounds (9 kilograms) more than everyone else; and Evered, who often competed with Figan for seniority. Faben, who once might have tried for the position, was not strong enough because he had lost the use of one arm.

Humphrey seemed to be the obvious choice to succeed Mike because he was so much bigger and stronger than all the others. However, Humphrey was intimidated by the teamwork of Hugh and Charlie. He may never have tried to take the position if something strange hadn't happened: Hugh and Charlie left the community.

The brothers had begun spending more and more time in the southern part of the range. Then they took a group of chimps from the Kasakela community and formed their own community in the south. It was called the Kahama community. This was the first time Goodall had ever witnessed a new community forming from an older community. Hugh and Charlie were out of the running to be alpha male, but the story of their separation would cause conflict between the two communities for years to come.

In January 1970, a few months after the split, Humphrey made his move. While Mike sat in Goodall's camp, eating bananas, Humphrey attacked him. Faben followed and joined in the ambush. The two worked together to beat up Mike, and then they left the scene. Mike had lost a battle and was now no longer in charge.

Humphrey took over the role of top-ranking male. Meanwhile, another battle was brewing as Figan and Evered were in a struggle to dominate one another. These two males had been playmates as infants, but now they were fierce rivals. One day, the two got into a fight high in the treetops. Figan fell from a tree and crashed to the ground, hurting his hand. He screamed out in pain. Flo, very old and frail, rushed to her son's aid. She calmed him and led him away from the fight. Figan stayed with Flo for three weeks while his wounded hand healed.

In 1972, just two months after rescuing and nursing Figan back to health, Flo's old body finally gave out and she died. For years, people all over the world had followed Flo's story through Goodall's articles, documentaries, and books. Now her story had ended. Her death touched the world. Flo is the only chimpanzee ever honored with an obituary in Britain's *Sunday Times* newspaper.

Flint was eight and a half years old when Flo died. He should have been able to manage on his own without his mother, but he was still very dependent on her. For three days after her death, Flint climbed the tree where he and Flo had shared their last nest. He stared at the empty nest for several minutes each day and then climbed down from the tree. As more time passed, Flint seemed increasingly lethargic and depressed. He refused to eat any food.

His body weakened and he fell ill. Finally, he crawled to the same spot where Flo had died, curled up, and died himself. Without his mother, Flint had simply lost the will to live. It was up to Flo's remaining children—Fifi, Faben, and Figan—to continue the story of Gombe's F Family.

Figan Takes the Top Spot

Despite being injured by Evered, Figan still pursued the position of alpha male. After he healed, Figan went after Humphrey, the alpha by then. The two fought, but neither chimp came out on top. Humphrey seemed weaker than before, but he had not yet lost the top spot. To help maintain his position, Humphrey formed a friendship alliance with Evered. The two chimps spent a lot of their time together. When Figan attacked, they were able to fend him off together.

Figan would not be able to beat the two strong chimps on his own. He would need a partner and ally, too. Soon after Flo's death, he got one—his brother, Faben. Although Faben would never be a leader because of his damaged arm, he was still a strong and powerful animal. Working together with Figan, the two were an unstoppable force.

In April 1973, the brothers made their move. They went after Evered, who raced up a tree. They charged the tree for more than an hour, but Evered finally managed to get away. Four days later, Figan went after Humphrey. It was evening and most of the chimps had settled into their nests. Figan was up in a tree feeding, but then suddenly something in his demeanor changed. He climbed down from the tree and climbed toward Humphrey's tree. As he moved, Figan's hair stood on end, bristling and making him look like a giant, angry balloon. He took off through the trees, violently shaking branches, and then leaped right into Humphrey's nest. The two big chimps wrestled and screamed. They fell from the nest, crashing to the ground 30 feet (9 meters) below. Faben stood some distance away, ready to help his brother if the need should arise.

Humphrey ran away, but Figan was not yet done. He continued to display wildly and shake branches. When Humphrey tried to make another nest, Figan attacked him again. Once again, Humphrey got away, but the result was a clear victory for Figan.

Humphrey was out, but Figan was not yet in as alpha male. Evered still posed a threat. One day, toward the end of May, Figan and Faben attacked him. The brothers worked together to chase Evered up a tree. For the next hour, they each displayed at Evered from the ground below, while Evered whimpered and cried. The F brothers had won the ultimate battle: Figan was Gombe's new alpha male.

Love and Change

In 1965, after she finished studying at Cambridge, Jane Goodall returned to Gombe along with her new husband, filmmaker Hugo van Lawick. Chimpanzee Flo had recently given birth to baby Flint. Goodall and van Lawick set up a banana-feeding station to keep the chimps nearby so that van Lawick could make a film about the new baby.

As time went on, more and more chimps learned about the plentiful bananas available at the banana station and came to take advantage of it. By providing the chimps with bananas, Goodall was able to interact with them more directly. They often came right up to her looking for a treat. This helped Goodall get closer to the chimps during her research, but the scientist later said that it was a mistake. She now believes that setting up the feeding station interfered with the chimps' natural way of life. Even more worrisome, it provided a setting where diseases could spread between chimps. The feeding station was removed in 2000.

Now that she was a leading expert in chimp behavior, Goodall was often called away from Gombe to speak with other scientists

Jane Goodall poses with her husband Baron Hugo van Lawick in March 1964.

or teach classes to college students. She no longer had the time to spend all of her days watching chimpanzees. However, there was still a lot to learn about the chimps' behavior, especially now that they were more comfortable with human beings. So, with a new grant from the National Geographic Society, Goodall and van Lawick set up the Gombe Stream Research Center. They invited students from all over the world to come to Gombe and help Goodall with her research.

Running the research center was a big change for Goodall. Whereas Gombe had once been a quiet retreat in which she did her work alone, it was now teaming with students eager to spend time with the famous scientist. It wasn't the only big change in Goodall's life: On March 4, 1967, she gave birth to a baby boy, Hugo Eric Louis. Goodall affectionately nicknamed him "Grub" after a kind of larvae from a beetle native to the area.

MOTHERHOOD

When Grub was a small baby, Goodall stopped doing most of the chimpanzee research herself and instead left it to the students. It wasn't safe to have a baby around the chimps. Because the baby was small and helpless, the chimps' natural instincts lead them to hunt him for food. There were other dangers from other animals, too. According to a 1977 *People* magazine article, Grub's first spoken sentence was, "That big lion out there eat me." Goodall did not want to take any chances. She or another adult stayed with the child at all times.

Goodall had another reason for spending so much time with Grub. She wanted to mother her child in the same way that the good chimpanzee mothers such as Flo did for their offspring. "I determined, having watched chimpanzee mothers loving their children and having such fun, I would do the same," she said in a 2009 interview with the nonprofit organization Academy of Achievement. Goodall also recognized the crucial role her own mother had played

Jane Goodall, her husband, and son "Grub" spend time together on the shores of Lake Tanganyika, where Goodall was filming the TV special, "The Baboons of Gombe," in 1974.

in her life. Based on her personal experience with her mother and the experience of observing chimpanzee mothers with their children, Goodall decided that she wanted to spend as much time as possible with Grub.

Fortunately, through her research at Gombe, Goodall was able to continue to learn about the chimps. Goodall had a little house built on the beach on the shores of Gombe. She spent her time advising students, writing articles, doing the administrative paperwork for the research center, and taking care of Grub. She did visit the chimps each day at the feeding station, but not for research purposes.

END OF A MARRIAGE AND A NEW LOVE

As years passed, Goodall and van Lawick began to drift apart. Goodall was busy running the research center at Gombe. She also had a job as a visiting professor at Stanford University in California. That meant that she had to leave frequently in order to teach her classes. Van Lawick was often away from home, too, taking assignments to shoot nature photographs and documentary films. The separation was hard on the marriage. In 1974, when Grub was seven years old, Goodall and van Lawick got divorced. Even though their marriage had not worked out, the two remained friends.

Goodall soon had a new man in her life. Derek Bryceson had visited Gombe in 1967 when he was the minister of agriculture for Tanzania. Goodall met with him and other officials to lobby to have Gombe named as a national park. Goodall later recalled having been scared before the meeting because she had heard that Bryceson was "mean and unsympathetic." The characterization couldn't have been further from the truth. He was deeply committed to protecting the wild lands of Tanzania. Gombe was named a national park in 1968.

Goodall's and Bryceson's paths crossed again in 1973. Bryceson was now the director of the Tanzanian national parks, of which Gombe was one. Bryceson and Goodall shared an instant connection and soon began dating.

Bryceson was an Englishman who was born in China in 1922. In 1939, he became a fighter pilot in the British Royal Air Force in World War II. During the war, Bryceson's plane was shot down and he suffered a spinal injury. He was almost completely paralyzed below the waist. Doctors told him that he may never walk again, but that didn't discourage him. For three years, the young man struggled to overcome his injury, eventually teaching himself to

A TRAGEDY CHANGES GOMBE

In 1968, Ruth Davies, an American student at the Gombe Stream Research Center, was following a group of chimpanzees into the forest. As the tape recorder she carried with her later revealed, she had been on the trail for a while and was tired. The ground she was walking on was covered with overgrowth that blocked the view of a cliff up ahead. Davies fell over the cliff and died.

Davies had loved her work studying chimpanzees. Her time at Gombe was among the happiest in her life. For this reason, Davies's parents decided that their daughter should be buried at Gombe. Goodall often visited Davies's grave. It became a place of quiet reflection for the scientist.

Davies's death caused Goodall to rethink the research practices at Gombe. Because the student had been in the forest alone, no one knew precisely where to look for her when she went missing. It took five days to find her body. After this tragedy, Goodall decided that a local guide must accompany all students in the forests of Gombe. That way, even if there was an accident, there would be another person to report back what had happened.

Goodall hired several Tanzanians to become field assistants, including Hilali Matama. The field assistants soon became a vital part of the Gombe Stream Research Center. In her 1986 book *The Chimpanzees of Gombe,* Goodall writes that the field assistants, "could provide research with an extremely important component: a core of individuals, with long-term commitment to the work, who were totally familiar with the chimpanzees, the terrain, and the food plants." While university students came and went, the field assistants remained. As time went on, they played an even more important role in Gombe's research.

walk with the use of a cane. He would continue to use the cane his entire life.

After the war, Bryceson earned a degree in agriculture from Cambridge University. When he finished school, he moved to Kenya and then Tanzania to become a farmer. He was one of the first white people to support Tanzanian independence and played a key role in helping to make it happen. He became an important figure in the government.

A Near-Death Experience

At the beginning of their relationship, Goodall lived at Gombe and Bryceson lived in the large city of Dar es Salaam. In order to spend time with one another, Bryceson flew a small single-engine plane out to Gombe. Due to his injuries, he could not perform the take-off or landing procedures on his own, so he always traveled with a pilot. Sometimes Bryceson and the pilot picked up Goodall and Grub and flew them out to visit other places around Tanzania.

On one such occasion, the four travelers were in the plane on their way to visit Ruaha Park. The pilot was flying the plane, and Bryceson was sitting with him in front. Goodall and Grub were in the back. Suddenly, smoke began billowing out from instrument panel of the plane. The pilot looked for a place to land, but there was nothing but rugged terrain for miles. They would have to take their chances and continue on to their destination.

After 45 minutes of flying, they came to a small landing strip. Just as the pilot was coming in for a landing, however, he saw a herd of zebras crossing the air strip. The pilot pulled back the plane and tried to land near some trees. The plane landed hard on the ground and its wings crashed into the trees.

The pilot opened the door and shouted that the plane might go up in flames. He then leaped out of the plane; Goodall and Grub followed closely behind. The door on Bryceson's side of the plane was stuck and would only open about two inches, so he could not get out that way. Furthermore, one of the plane's wheels had been

COLONIAL TANZANIA AND INDEPENDENCE

Prior to World War I, Germany maintained control of areas of East Africa now known as Tanganyika, Rwanda, and Burundi. Other European countries controlled other parts of the region. Many battles of the war were fought on these lands, displacing and killing the local people. An estimated 250,000 Africans were killed in Tanganyika during World War I.

After the war, the League of Nations (later replaced by the United Nations) took control of Germany's East African lands. It made Tanganyika a protectorate of Britain. While the British government did allow local Africans to govern themselves, it also encouraged large numbers of Europeans to move into the region.

In 1954, the Tanganyika African National Union (TANU), under the leadership of Julius K. Nyerere, began to campaign for Tanganyika's independence. Derek Bryceson supported Nyerere and the independence movement. In 1961, one year after Goodall arrived in Gombe, Britain withdrew and Tanganyika became independent. Nyerere won the election as the country's new leader in 1962. In 1964, Tanganyika came together with the island of Zanzibar to form one nation, Tanzania. The name comes from merging the first part of both names together.

destroyed so that the plane was sitting at a sharp angle. Goodall was worried about Bryceson. Given his paralysis, she didn't know if he would be able to make it out through the other door before a fire broke out. Bryceson remained calm, and he told Goodall that the plane was not going to catch fire. Slowly and with great care, Bryceson lifted himself out of the airplane.

No one was injured in the crash, but the ordeal was not over. In order to get to the park station, the group had to cross a crocodile-filled river. Luckily, they waded safely across with no trouble. Finally, they could relax.

Married Again

Before the plane crash, Goodall was unsure of her relationship with Bryceson. The two were in love, but both had been married before and each had gone through divorces just one year earlier. Goodall wasn't sure if she wanted to rush into another marriage.

Having a near-death experience made Goodall realize that she did not want to wait to marry the man of her dreams. Bryceson proposed and Goodall happily accepted. The two were married in 1975.

Tragic Times

After her marriage to Derek Bryceson in 1975, Jane Goodall continued to live at Gombe. She maintained her role as the director of the research center. Bryceson visited often from his home in Dar es Salaam and helped with running the center. There was a lot to do. At the time, Gombe had about 20 student researchers.

In May 1975, another tragedy struck: A group of 40 armed men raided Goodall's camp, captured four of the student researchers, and took them away by boat. There were three Americans and one Dutch student. Goodall did not find out about the raid until after it happened, and no one heard from the captors for weeks. Goodall worried that they had killed the students. The government ordered that Gombe be evacuated. Goodall, Grub, and others from Gombe went to Bryceson's house in Dar es Salaam and waited for news.

One of the hostages was released and was sent to the city to demand a ransom. The captors turned out to be political revolutionaries looking to overthrow the government of Zaire. The group demanded money, weapons, and political favors from the Tanzanian government to release the students. Because Bryceson had worked for the government, he knew that it would refuse to meet the demands.

Goodall felt terrible. She had invited these students to Gombe, and now their lives were in danger. She vowed to do anything she could to make sure the students were returned home safely. The

STAND-OFF AT STANFORD

In October 1975, Goodall traveled to the United States to teach one of her classes at Stanford University. When she arrived, she found that rumors had spread about the kidnapping. Goodall was shocked to hear that the money for the ransom had never been paid. People began saying that Goodall's husband and government officials would rather allow the students to be killed than pay the ransom. It was untrue. In fact, Bryceson had done more than anyone to secure the students' release. People also said that Goodall had failed as a leader. They said that she should have exchanged herself for the students. That would not have been possible, but this fact did not change people's opinions.

Some people suggested that Goodall leave the university, "just until things died down." She refused. Instead, she continued teaching. She gave media interviews and tried to explain her side of the story. During this time, Goodall's mother joined her in California. Late into the night, the two women would discuss the situation and how to deal with it. Goodall was glad to have her mother's support.

When the semester ended, Goodall left Stanford and her teaching position for good. Due to her efforts, most of the rumors had been quelled. However, Goodall was deeply disappointed in the way people had rushed to judge her before hearing her side of the story.

rebels finally agreed to negotiate with the American and Dutch embassies instead of the Tanzanian government. After weeks of negotiation, a ransom was paid. Two more students were freed, but one was still held. It took several more weeks for the final student to be set free.

The kidnapping took a toll on Goodall. She knew that the victims and their families had suffered deeply. Even though they were not physically harmed, they were damaged emotionally. Some people criticized her for not doing more to keep the students safe.

GRUB GOES TO SCHOOL

In 1976, when Grub was nine years old, Goodall decided it was time for him to attend school. Rather than have him go to school in Africa, Goodall sent Grub to England to live with Vanne. Grub stayed at the Birches and slept in the same bedroom where Goodall had grown up. His school was nearby.

REORGANIZATION OF GOMBE RESEARCH

Immediately after the kidnapping, the government of Tanzania barred non-local people from freely traveling to and from Gombe. Goodall and others needed to get special permission to visit the park. Students were not allowed to go there at all. The government was afraid of another kidnapping.

The government might have shut down the research center entirely if not for Bryceson. Because he had a good relationship with government officials, Bryceson was able to convince them to allow the research at Gombe to continue. He also helped to organize the local staff and keep the center going. The field assistants, including Hilali Matama, became an indispensable part of the research during this time.

Without students at Gombe, however, universities and other academic institutions would no longer provide funding for the research. In order to keep the research at Gombe going, Goodall set up a non-profit organization, the Jane Goodall Institute. The institute built a private fund to continue the research, which continues to this day.

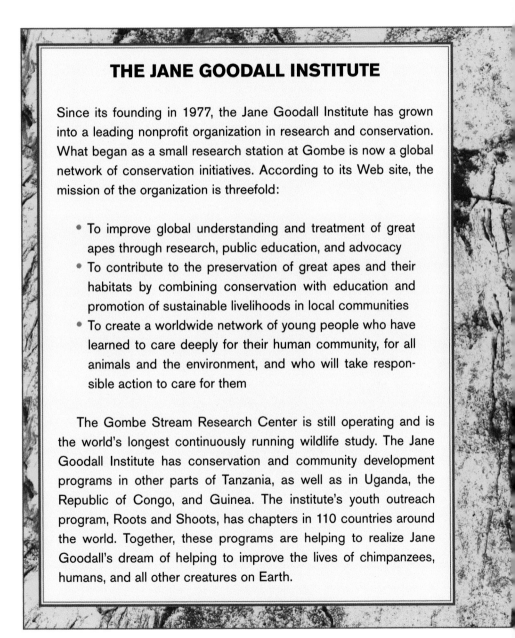

THE JANE GOODALL INSTITUTE

Since its founding in 1977, the Jane Goodall Institute has grown into a leading nonprofit organization in research and conservation. What began as a small research station at Gombe is now a global network of conservation initiatives. According to its Web site, the mission of the organization is threefold:

* To improve global understanding and treatment of great apes through research, public education, and advocacy
* To contribute to the preservation of great apes and their habitats by combining conservation with education and promotion of sustainable livelihoods in local communities
* To create a worldwide network of young people who have learned to care deeply for their human community, for all animals and the environment, and who will take responsible action to care for them

The Gombe Stream Research Center is still operating and is the world's longest continuously running wildlife study. The Jane Goodall Institute has conservation and community development programs in other parts of Tanzania, as well as in Uganda, the Republic of Congo, and Guinea. The institute's youth outreach program, Roots and Shoots, has chapters in 110 countries around the world. Together, these programs are helping to realize Jane Goodall's dream of helping to improve the lives of chimpanzees, humans, and all other creatures on Earth.

A GRISLY DISCOVERY

During this time of upset for Goodall's research station, there was also something deeply distressing happening in the world of chimpanzees. It started in 1971 when one of the researchers at Gombe witnessed a group of male chimpanzees attack a female from a neighboring community. They violently went after her and killed her infant. Then they did something unthinkable. They ate part of the infant's body. For the first time, chimpanzees had been observed engaging in cannibalism. Goodall and other scientists had known that chimpanzees sometimes hunted for other animals, but they had never before witnessed chimpanzee cannibalism. They thought it must have occurred in the heat of the attack and was not a part of normal chimpanzee behavior.

Chimpanzees can be very aggressive when confronted by animals—including other chimps—outside their community. Here, a male is angrily met by a mother protecting her infant.

Then, in 1975, another incidence of cannibalism happened. Goodall did not witness it herself, but later heard the story from her staff. One of the female chimps, Gilka, was sitting in the sun with her infant, Otta. Suddenly, two females from the community approached—Passion and her daughter Pom. Passion leaped onto Gilka and grabbed the baby. Pom jumped into the fray and helped to chase off Gilka. Then Passion bit into Otta's head and killed her. Over the next five hours, Passion and Pom fed on Gilka's infant as though she were any other prey animal.

Over the next four years, 10 newborn infants disappeared from the community. Goodall and her staff knew that Passion and Pom were responsible for six of the deaths and suspected that they were also responsible for the rest. After four years, Passion and Pom both had babies of their own. After that, the killing stopped.

Goodall has never figured out why Passion and Pom engaged in this behavior. It was very disturbing, and until recently it seemed to be an isolated occurrence. In a 2009 interview, Goodall revealed that Fifi and her daughter Fannie had been observed doing the same thing. The reason remains a mystery.

THE FOUR-YEAR WAR

In 1972, Goodall noticed that the chimpanzee community she was observing had split into two groups. The Kahama group, led by Hugh and Charlie, separated from the main group and moved to the southern part of the territory. The Kahama group was made up of seven males, three females, and their offspring, The Kasakela group, led by Humphrey, stayed in the northern part of the territory. When the two groups came across one another in the jungle, fights broke out. The fighting was a battle for territory.

In 1973, Figan took over as alpha male of the Kasakela community. In his new position, he led a series of attacks on the Kahama chimps. From 1974 to 1978 the Kahama and Kasakela chimps at Gombe were engaged in a civil war that came to be called the Four-Year War. The Kasakela chimps fiercely attacked the splinter group.

By the end of the war, the main group had wiped out the splinter group entirely. Only the adolescent females, who were of mating age, remained. They were accepted back into the original group.

For 10 years, Goodall had observed the wild chimpanzees of Gombe. She had come to believe that, although they had similarities to humans, they were generally kinder and gentler by nature. Suddenly, all of her perceptions had changed. She was reminded of her readings about the cruelty of human beings in charge of the Nazi concentration camps during World War II. Goodall has since come to understand that chimps, just like humans, have the capacity to be gentle and also the capacity to be violent.

A PERSONAL LOSS

In September 1979, Goodall's beloved husband began to have severe stomach pains. He made an appointment with the doctor. A series of tests revealed that Bryceson had cancer. Goodall and Bryceson left Gombe and traveled to London. They thought that the cancer could be removed with surgery, but the operation showed that the tumor was larger than expected. Bryceson was given three months to live.

The couple traveled to Germany to seek additional treatment for the disease. Goodall held out hope that there would be a way to save her husband's life. Over the next several months, however, Bryceson's condition worsened. On October 12, 1980, Derek Bryceson, the true love of Goodall's life, died. It was a dark time.

Taking Action

After her husband Derek Bryceson died of cancer, Jane Goodall felt deeply depressed. She had lost a very important person in her life, and she was unsure of what to do next. She returned to the one place that could help her heal—her beloved Gombe.

One morning, Goodall set off from her house in Gombe in search of chimps. She soon found one of her favorites, Fifi, with her offspring, Freud, Frodo, and Fannie. Goodall followed the chimps for hours, watching them climb from one tree to the next searching for food. She felt very peaceful and serene in the chimps' company. She was not there to study them, but rather just to enjoy their presence. She remembered her first days in Gombe and thought about how far she had come from those early days.

Lost in thought, Goodall did not hear the booming thunder of a large storm moving in. Suddenly, the sky opened and poured down great buckets of water. Goodall crouched under a palm tree to try and find some shelter. As she looked around, she noticed the chimps were doing the same. Together, chimps and human sat for more than an hour, waiting for the storm to pass.

When the storm cleared, Goodall and the chimps emerged from their shelter. Soon, more chimps came out from their hiding places to join the group. Goodall was drenched to the core and freezing cold, but she hardly noticed. She felt a great connection to the forest, the rain, and the animals around her—not only the chimpanzees, but also the birds, the bushbucks, and even the tiny spiders in their webs. Each had experienced the moment individually, but they had also experienced it collectively as a group.

In her 1999 book *Reason for Hope*, Goodall describes the experience this way: "I and the chimpanzees, the earth and trees and air, seemed to merge, to become one with the spirit power of life itself." In that magical moment, Goodall knew that her husband's death was just part of the great cycle of birth, life, and death that all creatures of nature experience. She knew that she would get through the tough times and be okay.

PUBLISHING THE RESEARCH

Goodall decided to stop wallowing in sadness and get to work. Over the years a vast amount of research had been collected on the Gombe chimps. Now it was time to compile the research and organize it for publication. Goodall wanted to do more than just publish her own data, though; she wanted to put that data into context with the other scientific data available. That meant she needed to do a lot of additional research. It was difficult work. Goodall had to learn about many complex scientific ideas before she could write about them.

There was another challenge: Goodall wanted her book to be easy for anyone to read, whether they were scientists or not. In an interview with the author of the 2006 book *Jane Goodall: The Woman Who Redefined Man*, Goodall said, "I'm reasonably intelligent and if I have to read something three times to understand what it means, why should I waste my time?" Making the book easy to read meant explaining difficult scientific concepts in a simple way.

Jane Goodall has been studying chimpanzee behavior in Gombe for more than 50 years.

Six years after Bryceson's death, Goodall finally completed her book. In 1986, *The Chimpanzees of Gombe* was published by Harvard University Press. It is more than 650 pages long. The book was well received by the scientific community and its completion was a great moment for Goodall. Years earlier, many scientists had dismissed her work. Now she was recognized as a leading primatologist and the expert on chimp behavior.

A CONFERENCE ON CHIMPANZEES

To celebrate the publication of her book, Goodall and Dr. Paul Heltne of the Chicago Academy of Sciences organized a conference titled "Understanding Chimpanzees." Scientists studying chimpanzees in different locations across Africa were invited to attend. Other scientists studying chimps in captivity were invited, too. The conference changed the course of Goodall's life.

At the conference, the scientists taught classes and talked about their own research. One of the classes was about conservation. Goodall attended and was shocked by what she learned. In that class, Goodall found out that the forests where chimpanzees lived were being destroyed at an alarming rate. By tearing down the forests, companies could build up the logging and mining industries and make way for roads and a growing human population and settlements. With fewer forests, the chimps had less habitat in which to live. The human settlements brought many problems. Because chimps can catch human diseases, the chimps caught more deadly diseases and spread them within their own communities.

The larger human population also meant a need for an additional food supply. People in some places in Africa have always eaten chimpanzee, or "bushmeat," but usually they hunted it themselves and only took what they needed to feed their villages. Now poachers were hunting chimpanzees in large quantities to sell for food. They also captured baby chimps and sold them to circuses, zoos, or as pets.

At the time of the conference, the wild chimpanzee population had shrunk from more than a million to fewer than 500,000. Today their numbers are fewer than 300,000. Chimpanzees are listed as endangered on the International Union for Conservation of Nature (ICUN) Red List of Threatened Species. It is estimated that they will become extinct in the wild within 15 years if something is not done about it.

A Class on Medical Research

In another class at the conference, Goodall learned about the conditions in which medical research chimps lived. The animals lived

TROPICAL DEFORESTATION

The area of Earth between the Tropic of Cancer in the North and the Tropic of Capricorn in the South is called the tropics. The tropics receive the sun's most direct rays, creating a climate that is perfect for a wide variety of plants and animals. Tropical forests cover about 7 percent of Earth's land, but they are home to more than half of its species.

Tropical forests across the globe, including in Africa, are being cut down to meet the needs of humans. This deforestation has a big impact on the animals that live there, such as chimpanzees. Many of the animals that live in tropical forests are endangered.

According to NASA, there is a common cycle to deforestation: Parts of the forest are cleared in order to build roads. The roads provide a way into the forest that wasn't there before. Then loggers move in to clear the trees and sell the wood, and farmers slash and burn the lands to plant crops or raise cattle. The nutrients from the soil dry up and the land becomes a desert, unable to support much life.

It may seem like there would be a simple solution to stop people from cutting down the trees, but there isn't. The people who live near the forests often depend on the agriculture in deforested areas to survive. When the nutrients in the soil dry up, they must move on to the next patch of deforested land in order to grow the food and raise the animals they need to live. In an April 2010 interview with the *Minneapolis Star-Tribune*, Goodall explained, "You can't expect people to care about trees if they're starving." In searching for a solution to help stop tropical deforestation, it is important to consider the people as well as the land and the animals. The following chapter will explain how Goodall is doing just that through her TACARE program.

alone in small cages, with no access to fresh air or affection. Even though she was not personally in favor of it, Goodall knew that medical research using animals was sometimes necessary. She certainly knew that it would not end anytime soon, but she was upset to learn that the animals were treated so poorly.

THE MYTH OF THE PERFECT PET CHIMPANZEE

Have you ever seen a baby chimpanzee dressed up in diapers on television or in an advertisement? It probably looked really cute, almost like a baby human. It is no wonder that so many people dream of one day having a pet baby chimpanzee. It seems like they would make the perfect pet, one that is cuddly, cute, and fun to dress up in human clothes.

Don't believe it. Chimpanzees do not make good pets at all. No matter how human they may seem, chimps are wild animals. They can never be completely trained or domesticated. As they grow from snuggly infants to adolescents, their bodies begin to mature. By age six to eight, they are five times stronger than a human being. They can often get frustrated because their natural urges are telling them to be out in a forest, not inside a home. This frustration can lead them to act out and behave aggressively.

In February 2009, a pet chimp named Travis attacked his owner's friend in Connecticut. The chimp was 14 years old and weighed more than 200 pounds (90 kilograms). As an infant, Travis the chimp had starred in television shows and commercials. He had lived with his owner as a member of the family and was

A Conservationist Is Born

Goodall felt she had to do something. After all, she was an expert on chimpanzees and a celebrity in the animal-scientist world. Surely she could use her name and her voice to help improve the plight of the chimpanzee. "It was a wake-up call for me," she wrote

treated just like a human child. In the attack, Travis destroyed both of the victim's hands, broke many bones in her face, and ripped off her nose, lips, and eyes. When police arrived at the scene, they shot and killed the chimp in order to save the victim's life. The victim lived, but her injuries will leave her disfigured for the rest of her life.

This chimp attack, which made national news, is far from the only incident of pet chimpanzees acting out. In fact, most of the baby chimps that people keep as pets, and even the ones you see on TV, are sold to badly run roadside zoos or animal laboratories when they become older and get out of control. The chimps cannot be returned to the wild because they are not equipped to survive there, and better zoos don't want them because they are not socialized to be around other chimps.

These chimps live out their long, 50-year lives in small cages. Meanwhile, more and more baby chimps are taken from their mothers to work in the entertainment industry or become somebody's pet. "Chimpanzees do not make good pets, but their fate is intimately tied to ours," Goodall wrote in a February 2009 article for the *Los Angeles Times.* If we can debunk the myth of the perfect chimpanzee pet, perhaps we can help stop the practice of breeding chimps for captivity and can help improve the lives of all chimpanzees.

in her 2009 book *Hope for Animals and Their World*. "I went to the conference as a scientist, planning to continue working in the field, analyzing and publishing my data. I left as an advocate for chimpanzees and their vanishing forest home." In a 2006 interview with *New York Times Magazine*, Goodall explained how the conference made her feel: "I knew that I could no longer sit in my beautiful forest. I had to come out and try and do something to help." Goodall understood that in order to save the animals she loved so dearly, she would have to leave Gombe and go out into the world to speak up for them, because they could not speak up for themselves.

300 Days a Year

After learning about the challenges faced by chimpanzees at a conference in 1986, Jane Goodall decided that she needed to help them. She left her home at Gombe, where she had lived for 25 years, and hit the road. She was determined to make a difference in the world.

Since that conference, Goodall has spent 300 days out of every year on the road. She has traveled all over the world and has never remained in one place for more than three weeks at a time. Even then, if she is in one place, she is usually working on a book or other writing. Goodall only returns to Gombe once or twice a year and only for a week or two at a time.

This may sound like a difficult way to live, and in many ways, it is. However, with her tireless efforts, Goodall has met with heads of state, local officials, and leaders of environmental groups to educate them about chimpanzees and convince them to take part in conservation efforts. She has established Wildlife Awareness weeks in many countries and has given lectures at schools, businesses, and in local communities. Goodall has been able to help chimpanzees

At one of her many school events, Jane Goodall hands out awards to students and teachers at Beijing 101 Middle School in China's capital city on September 18, 2010.

and other animals in remarkable ways. Her work is an inspiration to young people and to conservationists all over the world.

Along with the successes come disappointments. The environment is still polluted, the forests in Africa are still being cut down, and chimps are still being killed for the commercial bushmeat trade. Other people might become discouraged in the face of these disappointments, but not Goodall. She tries to focus on one word to keep going in her work: Hope.

SYMBOLS OF HOPE

Goodall always has hope that things will improve for the environment, the people of the world, chimpanzees, and all other animals.

When traveling, she carries around "symbols of hope" to share with the people she meets. These symbols include a feather from a California condor—a species that was saved from near-extinction—and a leaf from a tree that has survived through 17 ice ages and is still alive today. The stories that go along with these artifacts remind people, Goodall included, of why it is important to continue to work for conservation—and why one must never give up hope.

BIG ACCOMPLISHMENTS

In her 25 years as a conservationist, Goodall has succeeded in making the world a better place for animals. She has also worked to improve the lives of people in African communities. Below are just a few of her biggest accomplishments.

Chimpanzee Sanctuary

On one of her trips to Africa, Goodall saw a baby chimpanzee in a tiny cage at a public market. The chimpanzee was for sale in the live animal trade. Like many other baby chimps, its mother had most likely been killed, either for meat or as a way to steal the baby. It broke Goodall's heart to see this orphaned chimp looking up at her. She knew she had to do something.

Goodall decided to create chimpanzee sanctuaries for orphaned chimps. Sometimes the chimps are rescued from markets like the one Goodall visited, while other times they are handed over by people who kept them as pets. Since chimpanzees are much stronger than humans and can be aggressive, they become dangerous to have as pets after only a few years. Such chimps cannot be returned to the wild, because other groups of chimps will not accept them. They must be cared for their entire lives.

Many people warned Goodall not to create the sanctuaries. They thought it would be too expensive and that her resources would be better spent elsewhere. They considered the orphaned chimps to be lost causes. Goodall ignored that advice. In her 1999 book *Reasons for Hope*, Goodall writes, "I could not turn my back on the outstretched hands, the pleading eyes, the pathetic, malnourished bodies of the orphans." The Jane Goodall Institute's sanctuaries are places where orphaned chimps have plenty of land to roam and where they can live happily for the rest of their lives.

MR. H, MASCOT FOR HOPE

If you were ever to go see Jane Goodall speak in person, chances are she would have a stuffed monkey named Mr. H with her. Mr. H is Goodall's mascot, and he travels with her wherever she goes.

Goodall's good friend Gary Haun gave the stuffed monkey to Goodall as a gift in 1996. Haun is blind; he lost his eyesight at the age of 25. However, he has not let this physical obstacle stop him from accomplishing great things. After losing his eyesight, Haun decided to learn how to perform magic tricks. Many people thought it was a bad idea. They didn't think a blind man could be a good magician. Haun proved everyone wrong. He's not just a good magician—he's a great one. In addition to learning magic, Haun also learned to scuba dive, cross-country ski, and do karate. He speaks to young people about the importance of never giving up their dreams, no matter what obstacles are thrown their way

When Haun gave Goodall Mr. H, he thought he was giving her a stuffed chimpanzee, not a monkey. Goodall told Haun to feel for the tail because monkeys have tails, but chimpanzees do not. Regardless, Haun asked Goodall to carry Mr. H with her always as a symbol of inspiration. Goodall agreed.

To date, Mr. H has visited more than 60 countries with Goodall. Everywhere she goes, Goodall invites the people she meets to touch Mr. H for good luck. More than 2.5 million people have touched the stuffed monkey and have been inspired by Haun's story. Mr. H even inspired a line of "Mr. H, Jr." stuffed animals, the profits of which benefit the work of the Jane Goodall Institute.

Improving Zoos

When Goodall was a young woman, it was common for zoos, even in large cities, to keep the animals in small cages with no companionship and little or nothing to do. Since then, many zoos

Mr. H has become a constant companion for Jane Goodall as she travels the world. Here, she poses with him at an environmental conference in the Netherlands in June 2002.

have improved considerably. They now have more natural environments and have interactive activities to keep the animals engaged and active. In an April 2010 interview with Marianne Schall for *The Huffington Post*, Goodall said, "When you come to a really good zoo, where the chimps are in a group and the keepers understand them and love them . . . if I'm a chimp, that would be a good choice of habitat in which to live."

SANCTUARY SUCCESS: PETIT PRINCE

Petit Prince is just one of many chimpanzees at the Jane Goodall Institute's Tchimpounga Chimpanzee Rehabilitation Center in Congo. He is named for the main character in the French book *Le Petit Prince* (*The Little Prince*) by Antoine de Saint-Exupéry. In this book, a young boy goes on adventures throughout the universe. The little chimp called Petit Prince would have to learn to be on his own, too, so the name fit.

Petit Prince was rescued when he was just two months old. He had been tied up in a bag, his leg severely injured from being caught in a trap. When he arrived at the sanctuary, the caretakers got right to work fixing up his wounds and getting him used to his new home.

The little chimp quickly adjusted to his new life. He enjoys walking through the forest and observing the world around him. One day, Petit Prince was walking through the forest with one of his human caretakers. Suddenly, the little chimp became agitated and made a lot of noise. The caretaker looked down at the ground. Right in front of her was a poisonous snake. Petit Prince's actions had warned the caretaker to get out of harm's way. The incident reminded that caretaker that just as she is looking out for the chimps, sometimes they are looking out for her, too.

Unfortunately, it is expensive to maintain high-quality zoos. Many of the zoos in poorer countries are not able to afford the keep-up of good living conditions for the animals. The Jane Goodall Institute has worked with zoo owners in many of these places to help improve zoo conditions and the quality of care for the animals there.

ChimpanZoo Project

In 1984, Goodall started a project called ChimpanZoo to help collect data about zoo chimps, much in the same way Gombe's research is collected. "If we could collect data at a number of different zoos, using the same behavior categories we do at Gombe, and similar recording techniques, a whole new wealth of information would become available," Goodall explains in the 1999 book *40 Years at Gombe.* Thanks to the ChimpanZoo project, we now know more than ever about the particular needs of captive chimps. That information helps zoos all over the world improve their chimp enclosures and the animals' lives.

Research Chimps

In 1987, Goodall visited a medical research laboratory in the United States. As she toured the facility, she saw baby chimps kept in tiny boxes, called isolettes, which kept them isolated from other animals. One chimp named Barbie especially upset Goodall. Barbie cowered in the back of her cage, rocking from side to side.

After the meeting, Goodall developed a set of minimum requirements for the well-being of laboratory animals. The requirements were largely ignored at first, but Goodall persisted. Today, things are changing. Many laboratories have larger cages for their animals and allow them to interact with one another. Goodall hopes to reach a day when animal research is no longer necessary, but, until then, she will continue to work to improve the lives of research animals.

Helping People

Goodall knew that her efforts to protect the chimpanzees in Africa would be useless unless she could also do something to help the people in the communities there. After all, they were also dealing with the consequences of deforestation and diminishing numbers of wild animals. Goodall wanted to help the people in these communities to improve their own lives.

The Jane Goodall Institute established a program called TACARE to do just that. It started with 12 villages and has since expanded. The program teaches people about conservation and how to protect the land. It helps them plant tree nurseries and teaches them sustainable-farming methods. It also provides educational scholarships and business loans to people, especially young women, to make them financially independent. The program provides medical assistance, too.

In a 2003 speech, Goodall talked about the success of the program: "The people in these villages now realize we care about them as well as the chimpanzees. They support us in what we do. They are prepared to help us conserve the chimpanzees." With the support of the local people, the Jane Goodall Institute is able to do even more to protect the chimpanzees in the area. Both the chimpanzees and the people benefit. It is a win-win situation.

Awards and Honors

Goodall has received worldwide recognition for her work with the chimpanzees. She was awarded the San Diego Zoological Society's Gold Medal of Conservation in 1974, the Paul Getty Wildlife Conservation Prize in 1984, the Animal Welfare Institute's Schweitzer Medal in 1987, the National Geographic Society Centennial Award in 1988, and the Kyoto Prize in Basic Sciences in 1990. In 2002, she was named a United Nations Messenger of Peace and, in 2003, Queen Elizabeth II of England honored Goodall by giving her the title of Dame of the British Empire.

Inspiring Young People

Goodall knows that no matter how much she does to protect our planet, she can't do it all on her own. That's why she has enlisted tens of thousands of young people all across the globe to help. In 1991, Goodall established the Roots & Shoots program to encourage young people to work in their local communities to help people, animals, and the environment. On the Roots &

Jane Goodall displays her medal in February 2004, after receiving the title Dame of the British Empire from Queen Elizabeth II.

Shoots Web site, Goodall explains the meaning of the name of the group:

> Roots creep underground everywhere and make a firm foundation. Shoots seem very weak, but to reach the light, they can break open brick walls. Imagine that the brick walls are all the problems we have inflicted on our planet. Hundreds of thousands of roots & shoots, hundreds of thousands of young people around the world, can break through these walls. We CAN change the world.

There are Roots & Shoots programs in more than 120 countries worldwide, with tens of thousands of young people participating. That number grows larger every year. Members of each group choose the projects they want to do based on local needs and their own interests. They might clean up a local stream or park, start a recycling drive, raise money for the local conservancy, or educate people in their community about conserving energy. Individually, each of these projects makes a difference locally. Together, they make a huge impact globally.

JANE GOODALL'S MESSAGE OF HOPE

Goodall often meets people who are discouraged by all the bad news out there. They think they can't make a difference. They don't know how to get involved and make their mark. They think that their own small actions won't matter in the grand scheme of things. "People feel helpless because of the enormity of the problem, and so do nothing," Goodall said in an April 2010 interview with the *Minneapolis Star-Tribune*. People should not feel that way, she said, because in fact, "one action multiplied by a billion makes a huge difference. Every single day, every single one of us makes a difference, and we get to choose what it will be. Spend a little time each day thinking of the consequences of your choices—what you eat, what you wear, how you are affecting the world. That's how to make those small differences add up." If just one person turns off the lights every time he or she leaves the room, that might not have

A young chimp named Pola puckers up to kiss Jane Goodall at the Budapest Zoo in 2004.

a big impact. However, if hundreds of thousands of people all did the same thing, imagine how much electricity we could save each year! The actions of one person truly do matter in the world.

Goodall's advice to people who want to get involved in conservation is to look for projects that help their local communities. "You know the little saying, 'Think globally, act locally'?" Goodall said in a 2010 interview with *The Huffington Post.* "No, act locally first, see that you make a difference—then you dare to think globally." What she means is that it helps to start small so that you can see your success, and then build from there. If each of us did that, we could truly make the whole world a better place for people, animals, and the environment.

How to Get Involved

The following organizations provide more information about conservation and volunteerism.

Roots & Shoots

www.rootsandshoots.org

The Jane Goodall Institute's youth outreach program has chapters all around the United States. Each group chooses its own project to help the local environment, animals, and people. Check the Web site to find a chapter in your area.

Do Something

www.dosomething.org

Each of us can do something to make a difference in the world. The Do Something organization provides teenagers with the resources they need to put their ideas into action. This Web site is a great place to be inspired to start your own conservation project.

Go Green Initiative

www.gogreeninitiative.org

This group is aimed at helping schools start eco-friendly programs on campus. They help students, parents, teachers, and administrators come together to make school a greener, cleaner place.

Youth Service America

www.ysa.org

The goal of Youth Service America is to engage young people in volunteer work. This Web site is a great way to find out about volunteer opportunities in your area and to find new ways to contribute to your community.

Chronology

1934	Jane Goodall is born in London on April 3.
1939	Britain enters World War II on September 3.
1945	May 8 is celebrated as VE Day (Victory in Europe).
1956	On December 18, Goodall receives a letter from her friend Clo, inviting her to Kenya.
1957	On March 13, Goodall sets sail for Kenya aboard the *Kenya Castle* ship, and arrives in Nairobi on April 3, her twenty-third birthday.
1958	Goodall returns to England to prepare for her chimpanzee study.
1959	Louis and Mary Leakey discovery the "Dear Boy" fossil at Olduvai Gorge.
1960	On July 16, Goodall sets foot in Gombe for the first time. On October 30, Goodall observes David Greybeard eating meat; on November 4, she witnesses him using a tool.
1962	Goodall is accepted to Cambridge University.
1963	Filmmaker Hugo van Lawick travels to Gombe to film a documentary about her; Goodall's article "My Life Among the Wild Chimpanzees" is published in *National Geographic*.
1964	Tanganyika and Zanzibar come together to form Tanzania; Goodall and van Lawick marry.
1965	Goodall earns a Ph.D. in ethology from Cambridge University; van Lawick's film *Miss Goodall and the Wild Chimpanzees* plays on U.S. television; Goodall and van Lawick found the Gombe Stream Research Center.

1966	Dian Fossey begins a field research study of mountain gorillas in Congo (then Zaire).
1967	On March 4, Goodall gives birth to a son, Hugo Eric Louis, also known as "Grub."
1968	A student researcher at Gombe falls over a cliff and dies.
1974	Goodall and van Lawick divorce; the chimpanzee "Four-Year War" begins; Goodall is awarded the Gold Medal of Conservation by the San Diego Zoological Society.
1975	Goodall marries Derek Bryceson; four students are kidnapped from Gombe and are later returned safely.
1977	Goodall founds the Jane Goodall Institute.
1978	The chimpanzee "Four-Year War" ends; the entire splinter group of chimps is killed.
1980	Derek Bryceson dies of cancer.
1984	Goodall is awarded the Animal Welfare Institute's Schweitzer Medal.
1985	Dian Fossey is murdered in Rwanda.
1986	Harvard University Press publishes Goodall's book *The Chimpanzees of Gombe*; to celebrate the book, Goodall organizes a conference on chimpanzees and is shocked to learn about the extent of chimpanzee-habitat destruction; she vows to leave Gombe and focus on conservation.
1988	Goodall wins the National Geographic Society Centennial Award.
1990	Goodall is awarded the Kyoto Prize in Basic Sciences.
1991	Goodall founds Roots & Shoots, a youth outreach program.

1994	Goodall begins the TACARE program to help local people become involve in conservation and improve their own lives.
2002	Goodall is named a United Nations Ambassador of Peace.
2003	Queen Elizabeth II makes Goodall a Dame of the British Empire.
2010	Goodall celebrates the fiftieth anniversary of her first trip to Gombe.

Glossary

activist   Person who campaigns to bring about political or social change

advocate   Person who publicly supports a particular cause

anatomy   Branch of science concerned with the bodies of humans or animals

ancestor   An early type of animal, from which others have evolved

anthropologist   Scientist who studies human societies and their development

apartheid   A policy of segregation based on race

cannibalism   Eating the flesh of one's own species

captivity   A state of being held or confined

conservationist   Person who works to protect nature

credentials   Qualifications to do something professionally

deforestation   Practice of clearing trees from forests

DNA   Material that carries genetic information

domesticate   To tame an animal in order to keep it as a pet or farm animal

ethology   The study of animal behavior

excavate   To dig up something from the ground

gorge   Narrow valley between hills or mountains

grant   Sum of money given to an organization or individual in order to carry out a project or other activity

great ape   A large ape of a family closely related to humans

hominid   A primate of a family that includes humans and their fossil ancestors

hostage   Person held against his or her will in exchange for money or some other form of ransom

isolette   A container to hold an animal and keep it free from germs

matriarch   Mother who is the head of a group of descendents

native   Person born in a specific country

nutrients Substances that help nourish something so that it grows

observe To carefully and attentively watch something

paleoanthropologist Scientist who studies fossil hominids (the ancestors of human beings)

paleontologist Scientist who studies fossil plants and animals

poacher Person who illegally hunts animals

prehistoric The time before written records

primate A kind of mammal that includes monkeys, apes, and humans

primatologist Scientist who studies primates

protectorate A region controlled and protected by another country

ration To limit the use of a good during times of shortage

sanctuary A place of refuge or safety

socialize To teach someone to behave in a way that is acceptable to society

specimen An individual plant or animal used as an example of its species

taxidermy Preparing, mounting, and stuffing the skins of animals to make them look life-like

Bibliography

Biography.com. "Jane Goodall Biography." A&E Television Networks. Available online. URL: http://www.biography.com/articles/Jane-Goodall-9542363. Accessed August 10, 2010.

Encyclopedia Americana. "Tanzania." Grolier Online, 2010. Available online. URL: http://ea.grolier.com/article?id=0379270-00. Accessed August 10, 2010.

The Exploring 20th Century London Project. "1950–1959." Available online. URL: http://www.20thcenturylondon.org.uk/server.php?show=nav.43. Accessed August 10, 2010.

———. "Work." Available online. URL: http://www.20thcenturylondon.org.uk/server.php?show=nav.26. Accessed August 10, 2010.

Gavshon, Michael and Sarah Carter. "Fossil Discovery: New Link in Human Family Tree?" *CBSnews.com*. CBS Interactive, April 11, 2010. http://www.cbsnews.com/stories/2010/04/09/60minutes/main6379569.shtml. Accessed August 10, 2010.

Goodall, Jane. "Exclusive Interview with Dr. Jane Goodall." Interview by Marianne Schnall. *Huffington Post*. April 1, 2010. Available online. URL: http://www.huffingtonpost.com/marianne-schnall/exclusive-interview-with_b_479894.html. Accessed August 10, 2010.

———. *Hope for Animals and Their World*. New York: Grand Central, 2009.

———. Interview by Academy of Achievement. August 2009. Available online. URL: http://www.achievement.org/autodoc/page/goo1int-1. Accessed August 10, 2010.

———. "Loving Chimps to Death." *Los Angeles Times*. February 25, 2009. Available online. URL: http://articles.latimes.com/2009/feb/25/opinion/oe-goodall25. Accessed August 10, 2010.

———. "Medallion Speaker Address." The Commonwealth Club, October 10, 2003. Available online. URL: http://www.commonwealth

club.org/archive/03/03-10goodall-speech.html. Accessed August 10, 2010.

———. *My Life with the Chimpanzees*. New York: Byron Preiss, 1996.

———. "Q and A with Jane Goodall." Interview by Glenn Close. *Fetchdog*. July 1, 2009. Available online. URL: https://www.fetchdog.com/blogs/livelylicks/QandA/q_and_a_with_jane. Accessed August 10, 2010.

———. *Through a Window*. Boston: Houghton, 1990.

Goodall, Jane and Phillip Berman. *Reason for Hope: A Spiritual Journey*. New York: Warner, 1999.

The Jane Goodall Institute. "About JGI." Janegoodall.org. Available online. URL: http://www.janegoodall.org/about-jgi. Accessed August 10, 2010.

———. "About Us." Roots & Shoots. Available online. URL: http://www.rootsandshoots.org/aboutus. Accessed August 10, 2010.

———. "Introducing Petit Prince." Janegoodall.org, February 25, 2009. Available online. URL: http://www.janegoodall.org/media/news/introducing-petit-prince. Accessed August 10, 2010.

———. *Jane Goodall: 40 Years at Gombe*. New York: Stewart, Tabori, & Chang, 1999.

———. "The Story of Mr. H." Janegoodall.org. Available online. URL: http://www.janegoodall.org/blogs/story-mr-h-janes-traveling-companion. Accessed August 10, 2010.

———. "Study Corner: Biography." Janegoodall.org. Available online. URL: http://www.janegoodall.org/study-corner-biography. Accessed August 10, 2010.

———. "Study Corner: Jane Timeline." Janegoodall.org. Available online. URL: http://www.janegoodall.org/study-corner-jane-timeline. Accessed August 10, 2010.

The Jane Goodall Institute of Canada. "Jane Goodall: Biographical Timeline." Available online. URL: http://www.janegoodall.ca/goodall-bio-timeline.php. Accessed August 10, 2010.

Joyce, Christopher. "Odd Fossil May Be Human Ancestor or Dead End." NPR, April 8, 2010. Available online. URL: http://www.

npr.org/templates/story/story.php? storyId=125713226. Accessed August 10, 2010.

Kovler, Peter and Judy Lansing. "Jane Goodall & Derek Bryceson Share a Marriage and a Love of the African Wilds." *People.* October 24, 1977. Available online. URL: http://www.people.com/people/archive/article/0,,20069379,00.html. Accessed August 10, 2010.

Leakey.com. "Leakey Legacy." Available online. URL: http://www.leakey.com/leakey_legacy.htm. Accessed August 10, 2010.

Lickley, David, dir. *Jane Goodall's Wild Chimpanzees.* 2002. PBS. DVD.

Lindsey, Rebecca. "Tropical Deforestation." *Earth Observatory,* March 30, 2007. Available online. URL: http://earthobservatory.nasa.gov/Features/Deforestation/deforestation_update.php. Accessed August 10, 2010.

Marr, Andrew. "A Swansong to 'Olde Britain.'" Editorial. *BBC News Magazine.* May 22, 2001. Available online. URL: http://news.bbc.co.uk/2/hi/uk_news/magazine/6676967.stm. Accessed August 10, 2010.

Maxon, Robert. "Kenya." *The New Book of Knowledge.* Grolier Online, 2010. Available online. URL: http://nbk.grolier.com/cgi-bin/article?assetid=a2016090-h. Accessed August 10, 2010.

Mixon, Bobbie. "Ancient Nutcracker Man Challenges Ideas on Evolution of Human Diet." *U.S. News and World Report.* April 30, 2008. Available online. URL: http://www.usnews.com/science/articles/2008/04/30/ancient-nutcracker-man-challenges-ideas-on-evolution-of-human-diet.html. Accessed August 10, 2010.

Oprah.com. "The Will to Live." Harpo Productions, November 11, 2009. Available online. URL: http://www.oprah.com/oprahshow/Chimp-Attack-Victim-Charla-Nash-Shows-Her-Face/2. Accessed August 10, 2010.

PBS. "Jane Goodall's Wild Chimpanzees: Jane Goodall's Story." Available online. URL: http://www.pbs.org/wnet/nature/episodes/jane-goodalls-wild-chimpanzees/jane-goodalls-story/1911/>. Accessed August 10, 2010.

PBS Home Video. *Jane Goodall: Reason for Hope.* DVD. 1999.

Peterson, Dale. *Jane Goodall: The Woman Who Redefined Man.* New York: Houghton, 2006.

Silverleib, Alan. "Ancient Skeletal Remains Shed New Light on Evolution." CNN, April 8, 2010. Available online. URL: http://www.cnn.com/2010/TECH/science/04/08/hominid.discovery.skeleton/index.html. Accessed August 10, 2010.

Solomon, Deborah. "The Chimp's Champion." *New York Times Magazine,* July 16, 2006.

Tillotson, Kristin. "Jane Goodall: First Chimps, Now the World." *Star Tribune,* April 14, 2010. Available online. URL: http://www.startribune.com/lifestyle/style/10846059.html. Accessed August 10, 2010.

Weise, Hans. "From England to the Forests of Africa." Animal Planet. Available online. URL: http://animal.discovery.com/fansites/janegoodall/jane/bio/bio.html. Accessed August 10, 2010.

Further Resources

BOOKS

Bow, Patricia. *Chimpanzee Rescue: Changing the Future for Endangered Species.* Richmond Hill, Ontario, Canada: Firefly Books, 2004.

Goodall, Jane. *The Chimpanzees I Love: Saving Their World and Ours.* New York: Scholastic, 2001.

————. *My Life with the Chimpanzees.* New York: Byron Preiss Visual Publications, 1996.

Greene, Meg. *Jane Goodall: A Biography.* Westport, Conn.: Greenwood, 2005.

Haugen, Brenda. *Jane Goodall: Legendary Primatologist.* Minneapolis, Minn.: Compass, 2006.

Maynard, Thayne. *Working with Wildlife: A Guide to Careers in the Animal World.* London: Franklin Watts, 2000.

WEB SITES

The Jane Goodall Institute
http://www.janegoodall.org/youth
Read more about Dr. Goodall's life work and find out about how you can get involved.

Lessons for Hope
http://www.lessonsforhope.org/student/studentsJournal.asp
This Web-based class includes a photo scrapbook about Goodall's life and interactive, hands-on projects.

National Geographic Kids
http://kids.nationalgeographic.com/Animals/CreatureFeature/ Chimpanzee
This fun, interactive site is loaded with pictures, videos, and information about chimpanzees.

San Diego Zoo

http://www.sandiegozoo.org/animalbytes/t-chimpanzee.html
Learn more about chimps and their behavior with info from the San
Diego Zoo.

Picture Credits

Index

About the Author

TARA WELTY is freelance writer and editor. She began her career more than 10 years ago as a social studies editor for Harcourt School Publishers, and went on to work as an editor at Macmillan/McGraw Hill and Scholastic. She holds a master's degree in playwriting from the Gallatin School of Individualized Study at New York University and a bachelor's degree from the University of Central Florida. Much like Jane Goodall, Welty has always felt an affinity for animals. As a teen, meeting a sweet-natured cow (who she named "Joe") inspired her to become a vegetarian. Welty, her husband, and their two cats live in Brooklyn, New York.